Powerful Classroom Management Strategies

Paul R. Burden

Powerful Classroom Management Strategies

Motivating
Students
to Learn

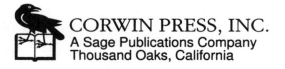
CORWIN PRESS, INC.
A Sage Publications Company
Thousand Oaks, California

For information:

Corwin Press, Inc.
A Sage Publications Company
2455 Teller Road
Thousand Oaks, California 91320
E-mail: order@corwinpress.com

Sage Publications Ltd.
6 Bonhill Street
London EC2A 4PU
United Kingdom

Sage Publications India Pvt. Ltd.
M-32 Market
Greater Kailash I
New Delhi 110 048 India

Printed in the United States of America

Library of Congress Cataloging-in-Publication Data

Burden, Paul R.
    Powerful classroom management strategies: Motivating students to learn / by Paul R. Burden.
        p.   cm.
Includes bibliographical references and indexes.
ISBN 0-7619-7562-4 (cloth: alk. paper)
ISBN 0-7619-7563-2 (pbk.: alk. paper)
    1. Classroom management.   2. Motivation in education.   I. Title.
    LB3013 . B876 2000
    371.102'4—dc21   99-050711

This book is printed on acid-free paper.

                03   04   05   06   7   6   5   4   3

Corwin Editorial Assistant: Catherine Kantor
Production Editor: Denise Santoyo
Editorial Assistant: Cindy Bear
Typesetter/Designer: Tina Hill
Indexer: Teri Greenberg
Cover Designer: Oscar Desierto

Contents

Preface

Powerful *Classroom Management Strategies: Motivating Students to Learn* is designed to provide comprehensive coverage of information about motivating students. Instead of offering hunches and impressions about ways to motivate students, the content is based on research and best practice (look at the extensive reference list at the end of the book). Yet the content is written and organized in a way that is easy to read, understand, and apply. The book carries a practical, realistic view of teaching, and its content is applicable for teachers at all grade levels—elementary, middle level, junior high, and high school.

After three introductory chapters, specific recommendations for ways to motivate students are organized around decision areas that teachers typically make—instruction, evaluation and recognition, and academic and behavioral expectations. This is followed by a chapter concerning the unique motivational needs of hard-to-reach students.

Pedagogical Features

A number of pedagogical features are designed to make the book more useful.

- *Teachers in Action case studies.* These descriptions by teachers at all grade levels show how they apply the concepts discussed in the chapters.
- *Summary tables.* Numerous tables outline the significant topics and recommended strategies in each chapter.
- *Discussion/reflective questions.* Questions at the end of each chapter promote discussion in a setting in which a number of people are considering the chapter's content.
- *Suggested activities.* A list of suggested activities is placed at the end of each chapter to guide the reader to investigate or apply the issues addressed.
- *Recommended readings.* An annotated list at the end of the book suggests readings for further enrichment.
- *List of references.* All sources cited in the book document that the information comes from research and best practice.
- *Subject and name indexes.* Thorough subject and name indexes help the reader locate information quickly.

Acknowledgments

Many people provided support and guidance while I prepared this book. A very special acknowledgment goes to my wife, Jennie, and children—Andy, Kathryn, and Alex. Their support kept my spirits up as I prepared the manuscript. Dona Deam, my secretary, was very helpful in preparing materials for the permissions. Alice Foster, my Acquisition Editor at Corwin Press, was encouraging and supportive from the start.

A number of teachers provided descriptions of their professional practice, which are included in the Teachers in Action features. Their experiences illustrate the concepts and bring life to the content. The teachers are Deleen Baker, Arlene Bekman, Diana Benzing, Lisa Bietau, Ruth Criner, Jerry Cross, Mike Edmondson, Jane E. Gurnea, Marilyn Gutman, Lynne Hagar, Carol V. Horn, Jackie Huber, Terri Jenkins, Greg Morris, Nancy Nega, Janet Roesner, Alicia Ruppersberger, Leslie Seff, Peggy Shields, and Becky Taylor.

I also thank the reviewers of the initial and final manuscripts for their thoughtful critique and useful suggestions:

Lisa Bietau
Manhattan Public Schools
Kansas

Deborah Kraft
Assistant Professor in Education
Villa Julie College
Stevenson, Maryland

Marvin Lynn
PhD candidate in Education
University of California, Los Angeles
Los Angeles, California

Nancy J. Meducci, PhD
Adjunct Professor, Behavioral and Social Sciences
El Camino College
Torrance, California

—Paul R. Burden

About the Author

Paul R. Burden is Assistant Dean and Professor in the College of Education at Kansas State University, Manhattan, where he has supervised student teachers and taught courses on teaching methods, classroom management and discipline, instructional leadership, and foundations of education. Previously, he was a middle-level science teacher in Buffalo, New York, and later earned his doctoral degree at the Ohio State University. He received the College of Education's Outstanding Undergraduate Teaching Award in 1999.

His recent publications include *Countdown to the First Day of School* (2000), *Methods for Effective Teaching* (1999), and *Classroom Management and Discipline* (1995), as well as *Establishing Career Ladders in Teaching* (1987). From 1986 to 1997, he served as the editor of *Journal of Staff Development*, a quarterly journal sponsored by the National Staff Development Council, and has presented more than 70 papers at regional and national educational conferences in addition to authoring 15 articles and 4 book chapters. He has been a presenter at more than 40 staff development programs and currently serves as a reviewer for several journals.

Married with three children, Dr. Burden enjoys traveling with his family and seeing his children participate in musical performances and sports. He can be contacted at Kansas State University, 17 Bluemont Hall, Manhattan, Kansas 66506; (785) 532-5595; burden@ksu.edu.

**CORWIN
PRESS**

The Corwin Press logo—a raven striding across an open book—represents the happy union of courage and learning. We are a professional-level publisher of books and journals for K–12 educators, and we are committed to creating and providing resources that embody these qualities. Corwin's motto is "Success for All Learners."

The Complex Nature of Motivation

Imagine that one of your students doesn't seem interested in the subject matter of your course. The student exerts minimal effort on classroom activities, seatwork, projects, homework, and tests. The student gets off task easily, bothers other students, and disturbs classroom order. It may be that there are many such students in your classroom and that you are searching for ways to get these students interested and engaged.

This is where motivation ties in. If you can motivate students, they are more likely to participate in activities and less likely to get off task and contribute to disorder. An effective classroom manager deliberately plans for ways to motivate students.

How does motivating students fit into an effective classroom management system? *Classroom management* refers to the actions and strategies that are used to maintain order in the classroom (Doyle, 1986). You need to address several issues to implement classroom management (Burden, 1995):

- *Getting organized*—preparing for the school year, organizing your classroom, and selecting and teaching rules and procedures

1

- *Planning for management*—planning for instruction with management in mind, planning for motivation, planning to address the diversity of students, and planning to work with parents
- *Conducting the class*—establishing a cooperative and responsible classroom, encouraging and reinforcing appropriate behavior, and managing lesson delivery

As you can see, motivation is one important part of effective classroom management. It involves more than simply praising a student, however. Student motivation will be affected by your selection of instructional content, your instructional strategies, the tasks that you ask the students to complete, the way you provide feedback, the means of assessment, and other issues. If students are motivated to learn, they will be less inclined to get off task and contribute to disorder.

Because motivation is a multifaceted issue, it is helpful first to examine some of the reasons for its complexity in an effort to gain some understanding of its principles. Most educators use the word *motivation* to describe those processes that can arouse and initiate behavior, give direction and purpose to behavior, continue to allow behavior to persist, and lead to choosing or preferring a particular behavior (Wlodkowski, 1984). Of course, teachers are interested in a particular type of motivation in their students—the motivation to learn. Teachers who ask questions such as "How can I help my students get started?" or "What can I do to keep them going?" are dealing with issues of motivation. Slavin (1997) suggests that motivation is the influence of needs and desires on the intensity and direction of behavior.

Before considering what processes or strategies you might use to arouse, direct, and maintain student behavior to learn, it is useful to examine three related factors. First, recognize the merits and limitations of relying on intrinsic and extrinsic motivation. Second, recognize that there are several theoretical views of motivation, each having implications for the types of strategies that you select. Third, recognize that information about motivation, curriculum, and instruction has implications for decisions you make in the classroom.

Intrinsic and Extrinsic Motivation

There are two broad categories of motivation—intrinsic and extrinsic. *Intrinsic motivation* is a response to needs that exist within the student, such as curiosity, the need to know, and feelings of competence or growth. Internal satisfaction that a student feels about a particular task is another aspect of intrinsic motivation. For example, some students might find activities involving movement to be intrinsically satisfying (Raffini, 1996; Reeve, 1996).

Extrinsic motivation is motivation from outside the learner and has to do with external rewards for completion of a task. Words of praise from the teacher, a privilege, and a higher grade on a paper or the report card are examples. The reinforcement practices of extrinsic motivation can be effective, but the excessive use of rewards may be decreasingly successful in new situations, may foster dependence on the teacher, and may undermine intrinsic motivation.

Make everything you teach as intrinsically interesting as possible, and avoid handing out material rewards when they are unnecessary. At the same time, give extrinsic rewards when you feel that they are needed (Lepper, 1983). Rewarding students for participating in an exciting activity is not necessary, but extrinsic rewards may be needed after an activity that students find less intrinsically interesting and satisfying. After mastering multiplication tables, for example, you might provide some extrinsic rewards.

← ───────────────────────────────── →

TEACHERS IN ACTION

Using Extrinsic Rewards

Diana Benzing, junior high school language art and resource teacher, Neola, Iowa

Sometimes, students are not affected by letter grades and may do the minimum to get by. To help increase student interest in accuracy and quality performance, I have awarded points that can be translated into tangible rewards in the classroom.

Points are awarded for passing daily work, quizzes, and tests. Daily work is given a percentile score, and then the student gets points for that work, rounded to the nearest 10 (e.g., an 83% results in 8 points). Double points are given for quizzes; triple points for tests. Points are awarded for completing major projects, such as book reports (50 points), passing weekly notebook binder checks (25 points), and even getting parents to sign notes or attend parent-teacher conferences. Parent attendance at parent-teacher conferences has reached nearly 100% with this method.

Students turn in points for stickers, snack breaks, free time used in an approved way, or other rewards. To minimize disruption, points are tallied and payoffs are given only on designated days.

Students keep track of their own points either on graph paper (one square per point) stapled inside a manila folder or on a ledger similar to a checkbook register with "income" and "expenditures" listed. Prices of rewards must start low so everyone can get a quick reward and slowly increase through time as students learn how to earn points. All students must be able to earn payoffs. If it turns into a competition for top points, less able and less motivated students will feel left out, which will defeat the purpose of the system. A point system can be a great way to get students to push themselves to higher levels of excellence, which will eventually allow them to begin to experience the intrinsic rewards of achieving excellence for its own sake.

Theoretical Views of Motivation

Many factors will determine whether students will be motivated to learn. Several theoretical views of motivation attempt to explain aspects of student interest: the behavioral view, the cognitive view, the humanistic view, and the achievement view.

Although no single view of motivation explains student interest, these interpretations provide insight on individual differences in student desire to learn. The four views of motivation to be presented can serve as the basis for motivating your students (Biehler & Snowman, 1997). Both intrinsic and extrinsic motivation are used with each motivational view described here; extrinsic motivation is dominant in the behavioral view, whereas intrinsic motivation is dominant in the cognitive view, the humanistic view, and the achievement view.

The Behavioral View

Behavioral theorists stress that individuals are motivated when their behavior is reinforced. Research has shown that people will exert greater effort with reinforcement (Robbins, 1997). Students are motivated to complete a task because they receive extrinsic or intrinsic rewards. For example, a student may complete the task without protest because the score so gained will contribute to a good report card grade and praise from the teacher and parents.

With the behavioral view of motivation, a person's internal cognitive needs are not as important as the reinforcers that are provided to control the behavior. Reinforcers are any consequences that, when delivered immediately following a response, increase the probability that the behavior will be repeated.

The Cognitive View

The cognitive view of motivation suggests that individuals are motivated to understand the world, to have control over their lives, and to be self-directed. Cognitive theorists stress that individuals are motivated when they experience a *cognitive disequilibrium* in which they try to find a solution to a problem. Cognitive disequilibrium occurs when students realize that they need to know more about a particular subject. For example, when using a computer to prepare a class report, students may have to prepare a table that includes columns of information. Cognitive disequilibrium is created when the students realize that they do not know how to prepare such tables. The students are motivated to find a solution to the problem—to learn how to compose such tables. People are also motivated by curiosity, an urge to explore, or simply an impulse to try something that is fun.

The cognitive view highlights intrinsic motivation, whereby students value learning for its own sake. Students try to achieve the intended benefit from every school task. They tend to exhibit a relaxed, persistent, task-oriented state to increase their understanding of a topic or their level of a cognitive skill. What has been learned may have been selected because it represented a problem of personal concern, so the learner is likely to benefit from and remember it.

Although cognitive theory holds promise as a means to motivate students, its major limitation is that it is difficult to arouse cognitive disequilibrium in all students. For example, after asking a question that you consider to be provocative and imaginative, some students will be aroused while others may not be interested at all.

The Humanistic View

The humanistic view of motivation suggests that individuals are motivated by a need for growth and the development of self. This view highlights intrinsic motivation. Perhaps the best known theory of motivation in this category is Abraham Maslow's (1954) *hierarchy of needs*. Maslow hypothesized a hierarchy of five needs because needs are different at different times: (a) physiological—bodily needs such as hunger, thirst, sleep, and shelter; (b) safety—safeguards from physical and emotional harm; (c) social—affection, belongingness, acceptance, and friendship; (d) esteem—self-confidence, prestige, power, autonomy, achievement, recognition, and attention; and (e) self-actualization—the drive to maximize one's potential, growth, and self-fulfillment.

In this hierarchy, deficiency needs (physiological, safety, belongingness and love, and esteem) must be satisfied before growth needs (self-actualization, knowing and understanding, and aesthetic) can exert an influence. When individuals have satisfied their lower, or deficiency, needs, they will feel motivated to satisfy higher growth needs. Behavior at a particular moment is usually determined by their strongest need.

Everyone seeks to meet deficiency needs, and you should do everything possible to see that your students' lower-level needs are satisfied. When deficiency needs are not satisfied, students may make poor choices that lead them to off-task behaviors. Satisfying deficiency needs leads to a sense of relief and satiation; satisfying growth needs leads to pleasure and a desire for further fulfillment.

TEACHERS IN ACTION

Showing That You Care Helps Motivate Students

*Jerry Cross, high school English teacher,
Knoxville, Tennessee*

Motivation may come from several sources. It may be the respect I give every student, the daily greeting I give at my classroom door, the undivided attention when I listen to a student, a pat on the shoulder whether the job was done well or not, an accepting smile, friendly banter in the hallways, a lollipop for a discouraged-looking student, or simply "I love you" when it is most needed. It may simply be asking how things are at home.

For one student considering dropping out of school, it was a note from me after one of his frequent absences saying that he made my day when I saw him in school. He came to me with the note with tears in his eyes and thanked me. He will graduate this year.

Whatever technique is used, the students must know that you care about them. But the concern must be genuine—the students can't be fooled.

One limitation of Maslow's hierarchy is that you may have difficulty identifying which particular needs your students are lacking. Nevertheless, when trying to increase motivation to learn, you should have some understanding of your students' most significant needs.

For example, social needs of belongingness, acceptance, and friendship are important to students. You should take actions to help students meet these needs. Pursuing an invitational approach to education, as proposed by Purkey and Novak (1996), is one way to address these belongingness needs. *Invitational education* is a self-concept approach to the teaching and learning in which places, policies, programs, and actions are designed to invite development, promote cooperative activity, and treat people with dignity and respect.

With the humanistic view to motivation, a teacher is willing to adjust the curriculum to better meet the needs and interests of the students. In addition, a teacher listens to students for their ideas and feedback and also would likely try to see curriculum and instruction from the students' point of view when making instructional decisions.

The Achievement View

The achievement view organizes the reasons people have for wanting to achieve something. These reasons might include meeting personal needs to achieve success and avoid failure. By knowing why your students want to achieve, you will be better able to select instructional strategies that will promote their motivation to learn.

Maslow's distinction between safety and growth choices is similar to the concept of *level of aspiration,* which stresses that people tend to want to succeed at the highest possible level while at the same time avoiding the possibility of failure. When students are successful, they tend to set realistic goals for themselves, and successful experiences strengthen a need for achievement. But some individuals may experience a *fear of success*—they worry that being successful may interfere with positive relationships with others.

Some interesting aspects of success and failure are revealed when students are asked to explain why they did or did not do well on a task. The four most common reasons had to do with ability, effort, task difficulty, and luck (Weiner, 1979). The *attributional theory of student motivation* refers to students' attributing success or failure to these factors. The following examples illustrate student statements.

Table 1.1 Theoretical Views of Motivation

1. *The Behavioral View*

   A person's internal cognitive needs are not as important as the reinforcers that are provided to control the behavior. Individuals are motivated when their behavior is reinforced.

2. *The Cognitive View*

   People are motivated to understand the world, to have control over their lives, and to be self-directed.

3. *The Humanistic View*

   People are motivated by a need for growth and the development of self. This view highlights intrinsic motivation.

4. *The Achievement View*

   People are motivated to achieve something, such as the need to achieve success and to avoid failure.

- "I never do well on grammar tests." (ability)
- "I did not have time to study last night." (effort)
- "The test was too hard and too long." (task difficulty)
- "I guessed wrong about which sections of the book to study." (luck)

Low achievers attribute failure to lack of ability, and success to luck. High achievers attribute failure to lack of effort, and success to effort and ability. To enhance motivation and achievement, you may need to include ways of altering perceived causes of performance. Low-achieving students often seem to underestimate the amount of time and effort that high-achieving students put into their work. Persistence and problem-solving skills would likely help low-achieving students.

Table 1.1 summarizes the four theoretical views of motivation.

Implications for Teaching

Because you are interested in students' motivation to learn, several principles for teaching can be drawn from what is known about motivation, teaching, and learning. Each principle has implications for decisions you make concerning curriculum and instruction (Svinicki, 1991).

Principle 1. If information is to be learned, it must first be recognized as important. There is a higher probability of learning when students see the relevance of the content and when time is spent in learning the content.

Principle 2. During learning, learners act on information in ways that make it more significant, relevant, and practical. There is a higher probability of learning when the teacher and students use examples, images, elaborations, and connections to prior knowledge to increase the significance of the information.

Principle 3. Learners store information in long-term memory in an organized fashion related to their existing understanding of the world. Teachers can facilitate the organization of new material by providing an organizational structure, particularly one with which students are familiar, or by encouraging students to create such structures. At the start of a lesson, for example, advance organizers can help students understand the larger issues and see how that day's lesson fits into the larger picture (e.g., Parks & Black, 1990, 1992).

Principle 4. Learners continually check understanding, which results in refinement and revision of what is retained. Teachers can provide opportunities for checking and diagnosis to help students learn the content. Feedback and self-evaluation are important parts of instruction.

Principle 5. Transfer of learning to new contexts is not automatic but results from exposure to multiple applications. Providing several opportunities for students to examine the content helps promote understanding and the application of the content into new contexts. These opportunities can be in various instructional approaches and ways of grouping students.

Principle 6. Learning is facilitated when learners are aware of their learning strategies and monitor their use. Teachers can help students learn how to study and how they learn.

Summary of Main Points

- *Motivation* is the process of arousing, directing, and maintaining behavior.
- *Classroom management* refers to the actions and strategies that are used to maintain order in the classroom.
- *Intrinsic motivation* is a response to needs that exist within the student, such as curiosity, the need to know, and feelings of competence or growth. Intrinsic motivation may also involve the internal satisfaction that the student feels when performing the task.
- *Extrinsic motivation* refers to motivation that comes from outside the learner and involves the delivery of external rewards when a student completes a task. The reward might be words of praise from the teacher, a higher grade, or a privilege.
- Several theoretical views of motivation attempt to explain aspects of student interest: the behavioral view, the cognitive view, the humanistic view, and the achievement view.
- Several principles for teaching can be drawn from what is known about motivation, teaching, and learning. Each principle has implications for decisions you make concerning curriculum and instruction.

Discussion/Reflective Questions

- During the times when you were a learner in a classroom (K-12 or college), what types of intrinsic and extrinsic motivation were the most effective for you?
- If you were teaching an 11th-grade course on contemporary political issues, how might you satisfy the students' intrinsic needs (the need to satisfy curiosity, the need to know, the need

for feelings of competence and growth, and the need to be physically active) through your selection of the content, instructional strategies, and requirements for completion? How can you simultaneously accommodate students' individual differences, such as varied interests, knowledge, skills, and learning style preferences?

- Which theoretical view of motivation dominates your teaching? Why?

Suggested Activities

- List some extrinsic rewards that you use regularly and occasionally in your classroom.
- List some activities or approaches you have used in your classroom that the students have found intrinsically motivating.
- Think of a student who is hard to motivate, and consider which theoretical view of motivation would work best with that student.
- Interview one or more colleagues to discuss their approaches to motivation.
- For each teaching principle mentioned at the end of this chapter, list implications for your own teaching.

2

Motivating Students to Learn

Motivation to learn is a student's tendency to find academic activities significant and worthwhile and to try to get the intended learning benefits from them (Brophy, 1997). Although intrinsic motivation is primarily an affective response to an activity, motivation to learn is primarily a cognitive response involving attempts to make sense of the activity, understand the knowledge it develops, and master the skills it promotes (Brophy, 1997; Brophy & Kher, 1986).

To provide a framework for selecting strategies for motivating students to learn, this chapter explores the following:

1. Have a learning orientation in your classroom
2. Apply four strategies to promote learning
3. Bring the lesson to the students; bring the students to the lesson
4. Recognize the teacher's role in motivation

Have a Learning Orientation in Your Classroom

How students perceive their assigned tasks influences their motivation to learn as well as their perceptions of themselves as learners (Ames, 1992). In some classrooms, the main goal appears to be to complete the work to achieve a reward or simply to move on to the next task—this is a work orientation. In other classes, however, instructional goals are centered on learning and understanding the material—this is a learning orientation (Blumenfeld, Puro, & Mergendoller, 1992; Marshall, 1988, 1992, 1994). Teachers are largely responsible for establishing the orientation in their classroom. Clearly, a learning orientation is preferred.

It may be useful to look at these concepts as a continuum, with one end of the continuum being the work orientation and the other end being the learning orientation. Some classrooms may fall on the continuum at one end or the other. In practice, however, it is likely that many classrooms are actually a combination of these two orientations, depending on a variety of factors, such as the subject matter and student interests and abilities.

A Work Orientation

Teachers who promote a work orientation focus primarily on task completion, rather than learning. Teachers stress completing the work within the stated time limits when introducing activities, emphasize competition rather than cooperation among students, and give the correct answers following errors but do not use errors as occasions for helping students overcome their difficulties in learning. Students in work-oriented classrooms are seen as workers who produce worksheets under the watchful eye of the teachers as managers (Marshall, 1994). Their teachers make frequent reference to "the work" and the need to get the work finished and often have students use worksheets and workbooks. As a result, work-oriented teachers inadvertently create a threatening environment in which students are forced to try to cope with task demands, without much help from the teacher or classmates but with the knowledge that mistakes could trigger low grades and perhaps public embarrassment.

Students in work-oriented classrooms view assignments as tasks to be completed so they can receive a reward or privilege. They try to look smart, protect their egos, and learn only as a means to display superiority or avoid looking stupid (Nicholls, 1983; Nicholls, Cobb, Wood, Yackel, & Patashnick, 1990). In these classrooms, students frequently do not understand the purposes of academic activities, and they engage in these activities using surface-level, rather than deeper-level, information-processing and retention strategies.

Students in work-oriented classrooms may treat instructional tasks more as a test of their ability to perform than as an opportunity to learn. The students' primary concern is preserving their self-perceptions and public reputations as capable individuals. In striving to meet task demands and to avoid failure, students may rely on rereading, memorizing, guessing, and other surface-level learning strategies instead of deeper-level knowledge construction strategies. Their learning efforts may be impaired by fear of failure or other negative effects.

Students may avoid challenging tasks and tend to give up easily when frustrated because they believe that their abilities are limited, so they lack confidence that persistent efforts will eventually pay off. Rather than ask for help when they need it, they prefer to conceal their difficulties by leaving items blank, taking wild guesses, and perhaps copying from neighbors. In response to work that is too hard, students in work-oriented classrooms often try to get the teacher to lower the cognitive demands (Doyle, 1983) or to do the difficult parts for them (Marshall, 1987), rather than attempt to learn what the task is intended to teach.

Although many children enter school with a learning orientation or the desire to master something new, the teacher's use of extrinsic rewards, public comparative evaluation, ability grouping, and emphasis on visible products actually creates a work orientation in many classroom (Ames, 1990).

A Learning Orientation

Teachers who develop a learning orientation in their classrooms frame lessons with regard to what students will learn from the assignment and emphasize the importance of thinking and understanding, instead of focusing on "right answers" and completed worksheets (Marshall, 1994). Emphasis is placed on the learning purposes of schools and assignments and on the effort and strategies required to figure things out.

Teachers in learning-centered classrooms tend to speak of purposeful and reflective learning, and their curricula often include more open-ended and authentic tasks (Marshall, 1994). Teachers who foster a learning orientation create supportive environments that encourage students to engage in academic activities reflectively and often collaboratively.

Students in these classes try to understand and master something new or to gain insight or skill in something that is personally challenging, and they come to see themselves as learners and problem solvers. Students tend to see difficult tasks as a challenge and to choose challenging tasks over easy ones.

Students in classrooms with a learning orientation are more likely to focus on acquiring the knowledge and skills that the activities are designed to develop. They try to construct accurate understandings by paraphrasing the material in their own words and connecting it to prior knowledge. When they encounter difficulties, they are likely to seek help or, if necessary, to persist in their own self-regulated learning efforts because they believe these efforts are worthwhile and have confidence that the efforts will pay off eventually.

A learning orientation not only increases the time that children spend on learning tasks (Butler, 1987) and their persistence in the face of difficulty (Elliott & Dweck, 1988) but, more important, improves the quality of student engagement in learning. A learning-goal orientation promotes a motivational pattern likely to foster long-term and high-quality involvement in learning (Ames, 1992).

A review of the roles of teachers and students in work-oriented and learning-oriented classrooms is shown in Table 2.1.

Apply Four Strategies to Promote Learning

Phyllis Blumenfeld and her colleagues (1992) developed a concept of student motivation to learn, which they described as combining motivation and cognitive engagement. They compared fifth- and sixth-grade science classes in which students reported higher levels of motivation to learn with classes that reported lower levels of motivation.

Table 2.1 Classroom Learning Orientations

---

1. *A Work Orientation*

   Teachers in work-oriented classrooms

   - Focus on task completion and getting the work done
   - Emphasize completing the work within the time limits
   - Emphasize competition
   - Give correct answers after mistakes
   - See students as workers

   Students in work-oriented classrooms

   - Treat tasks more as a test of their ability to perform than an opportunity to learn
   - View assignments as tasks to be completed, often for some reward
   - Try to look smart and protect their egos
   - Use surface-level learning approaches (rereading, memorizing, and guessing)
   - May avoid challenges and give up easily when frustrated
   - May conceal their difficulties rather than seek help
   - May try to get the teacher to lower expectations of them

2. *A Learning Orientation*

   Teachers in learning-oriented classrooms

   - Frame lessons with regard to what students will learn
   - Emphasize the importance of thinking and understanding
   - Emphasize the effort and strategies required to figure things out
   - Often have more open-ended and authentic tasks
   - Create a supportive environment to help students reflect and collaborate

   Students in learning-oriented classrooms

   - Try to understand and master something new
   - See themselves as learners and problem solvers
   - See difficult tasks as challenges and choose them over easy tasks
   - Are willing to seek help or to persist in their own efforts

---

In the classes with the higher levels of motivation to learn, teachers stressed ideas rather than facts, highlighted the value of science through stories about scientists or about how science connects to everyday events, and expressed their own enthusiasm for the subject by relating stories of their personal scientific experiences. These teachers also made conceptual material more concrete and interesting by providing examples and by connecting the material to their students' experiences or to current events. They assigned more varied tasks and encouraged students to cooperate in small groups. In contrast, in science classes in which students reported lower motivation to learn, the teachers focused more on recitation, quizzes, and grades.

Four factors characterized the teachers' practices in the classes in which students reported higher levels of motivation to learn (cognitive engagement). These findings are consistent with other studies on motivation to learn. To help promote learning and maintain student motivation to learn, you should incorporate all four of these strategies into your classroom: (a) Provide opportunities to learn, (b) press students to think, (c) support students' attempts to understand, and (d) evaluate student learning.

Provide Opportunities to Learn

The teachers (a) focused lessons around midlevel concepts that were substantive but not overwhelming to students; (b) made the main ideas evident in presentations, demonstrations, discussions, and assignments; (c) developed concepts by presenting concrete illustrations of scientific principles and relating unfamiliar information to their students' personal knowledge; (d) made explicit connections between new information and things that students had learned previously and pointed out relationships among new ideas by stressing similarities and differences; (e) elaborated extensively on textbook readings rather than allowing the book to carry the lesson; (f) guided students' thinking when posing high-level questions; and (g) asked students to summarize, make comparisons between related concepts, and apply the information they were learning. Collectively, these approaches provided students with frequent opportunities to learn along with any needed assistance.

TEACHERS IN ACTION

Opportunities to Learn Through Discovery and Engagement

Marilyn Gutman, high school mathematics teacher, Las Cruces, New Mexico

I like to teach mathematics as a series of projects that actively challenge and involve students in guided discovery of the concepts. I often rewrite textbook lessons as multifaceted problems that students investigate in small groups. Each student tries to understand the problem through modeling activities, defines the problem in mathematical terms, and considers previous learnings to come up with a solution. Students then explain it to others and often write a report.

For example, many of my students have trouble remembering formulas. After building a castle of sugar cubes, Alan and Juan understood the meaning of area and identified several formulas to determine the areas of each part and the whole castle. By flattening a soccer ball for a pattern to tile a floor, María and Dora derived a formula for angles of a polygon. Velocity and acceleration had significance after a lab in which toy cars were rolled down a ramp. Modular arithmetic came alive through the study of secret codes.

The trick is to get everyone to actively investigate part of the problem and then become an important contributor in the "debriefing" session, which leads the group to discover the solution to the problem.

Press Students to Think

The teachers pressed for thinking through their feedback and expectations for lesson participation. They (a) required students to explain and justify their answers and held students accountable for their thinking; (b) prompted, reframed the question, or broke it into smaller parts when students were unsure and probed students when their understanding was unclear; (c) monitored for comprehension, rather than procedural correctness, during activities and checked for understanding; (d) encouraged responses from all students through such techniques as asking for votes or for students to compare their responses and debate the merits of different ideas (rather than allowing a small subgroup to dominate the lessons); and (e) supplemented the short-answer assignment in the commercial workbooks by adding questions that required their students to write explanations of results or alternative representations of information in the form of diagrams or charts. Through these approaches, students were required to actively think about what they were studying, instead of just monitoring the content passively or trying to memorize it.

Support Students' Attempts to Understand

These teachers supported their students' attempts to understand through modeling and scaffolding. They (a) modeled thinking, suggested strategies, and worked with students to solve problems when the students had difficulty (instead of just providing the correct answers); (b) reduced the procedural complexity of manipulative tasks by demonstrating procedures, highlighting problems, providing examples, and allowing for planning time; and (c) encouraged collaborative efforts by requiring all students to make contributions to the group. The teachers gave students whatever help they needed to enable them to meet the instructional demands.

Evaluate Student Learning

These teachers' evaluation and accountability systems emphasized understanding and learning rather than work completion, performance, comparison, or right answers. They used mistakes as ways to help students check their thinking, and they explicitly encouraged students who had done poorly to redo assignments or retake quizzes.

Bring the Lesson to the Students;
Bring the Students to the Lesson

With the objective of motivating students to learn, plan each lesson so that students have opportunities to learn during the lesson—bring the lesson to the student. During the lesson, students should be required to think about and use the content in some way—bring the students to the lesson (Blumenfeld et al., 1992).

Bring the Lesson to the Students

Bringing the lesson to the students can be done by providing opportunities for students to learn and by enhancing the interest value of the learning for students. You can maximize students' opportunities to learn by presenting material organized around concepts and by actively structuring material in ways that make these concepts clear and understandable for students. Students are able to understand material better when its relationship to their own experiences and to prior knowledge is apparent and when new ideas are presented in an organized manner using examples, explanations, summaries, and activities.

In addition, you should include content and activities in the lesson to enhance students' interest in the material being covered and to help them recognize the value of the content. You also should support students' cognitive efforts to learn and understand and should maintain a task focus by holding students accountable for participation and careful thought.

TEACHERS IN ACTION
Lesson Involvement Through Debates

Carol V. Horn, sixth-grade teacher,
Fairfax County, Virginia

Of all the activities that I use to engage my students, they seem to enjoy debates the most. We have them at least once a month, with three topics being debated each time to provide an opportunity for everyone to participate. Topics are generated through brainstorming, and a majority vote determines the three topics that will be debated that month. The debates cover a broad spectrum of issues, ranging from cloning to diplomatic immunity to school uniforms. Each debate involves two 5-member teams. To determine team members, I randomly call student names (using a cup of Popsicle sticks with a name on each stick). When called, each student can select the debate topic and a pro or con side to that topic. This process is followed until all teams are complete.

The teams then meet, choose a chairperson, and set up a time frame in which to research their issue and form their arguments. One person from each side works on an additional team to create a scoring sheet, setting up criteria to be evaluated and points to be awarded by the audience during the debate. As the year progresses, they learn the importance of having evidence to support their opinions, speaking clearly and confidently, and using persuasive language. They refine the scoring sheets as they become more aware of the essential skills needed to win a good debate. They also become adept at using the Internet, surveys, interviews, and other sources to find supporting information. Thinking and reflecting become important components as students explore issues from opposing sides, identify key aspects, and create speeches to persuade the audience that their argument is stronger.

Thinking during the debates adds an additional challenge. Students must listen carefully to each other's speeches and then form questions that will weaken the other team's position. The rebuttal is probably the most difficult because they have to listen closely and then speak extemporaneously about the other person's argument. They seem to enjoy the competitive nature of the debates, and it is interesting to note that as the year progresses and their skills improve, the final vote from the audience becomes a lot closer.

Student interest and enthusiasm are evidence of the importance of having opportunities to engage in stimulating and challenging discourse about topics that are of genuine interest to them. The debates are engaging, have a real-world connection, provide time for interaction and planning, and teach students to value and defend their ideas. Debates are an excellent strategy for promoting and nurturing a thinking classroom.

Bring the Students to the Lesson

Bringing the students to the lesson can be done by requiring students to think about and use the material and by supporting their efforts to do so. To bring the students to the lesson and to promote cognitive engagement, plan for widespread participation through questions and feedback, activities, assignments, and guided practice.

You can encourage students to become actively engaged in the lesson through questions designed to check for comprehension of the concept under discussion and to determine whether students can apply the concept to new situations and identify links with other ideas. Feedback that requires justification and explanation provides opportunities for students and teachers to examine and diagnose students' thinking.

Activities can promote motivation by posing a problem, being novel, and allowing students to exercise some choice and control. To promote cognitive engagement, activities must also require students to synthesize, represent, demonstrate, and apply their knowledge in a variety of ways, not merely arrive at the right answer.

Supporting students' efforts to understand is an important part of bringing the students to the lesson. By supporting their efforts to learn, students can meet high-level intellectual demands without being overwhelmed by frustration and confusion.

You can use several ways to support students' efforts to learn. For example, you could (a) sequence the material and questions so that students have information relevant to answer high-level questions, (b) make tasks manageable by breaking them down into smaller parts, (c) provide models and examples, and (d) reduce the complexity of procedures necessary to complete tasks. When using small groups for instruction, allow time for groups to plan, share, and reflect on what they have done. All these practices reduce confusion and help students feel capable of completing the assigned task and solving problems they encounter. In so doing, these practices enhance students' abilities to be successful.

Recognize the Teacher's Role in Motivation

Teachers need to develop a positive motivational orientation in students. In doing so, it is important to recognize that motivation occurs in a context—in the school and the classroom. A comprehensive approach is needed when looking at how motivational theory and research can guide classroom practice. When developing a comprehensive approach to motivational planning, Carole Ames (1990) maintains that three things need to be taken into account:

1. Any motivational plan should focus on motivating students to learn.
2. A framework is needed for identifying the aspects or structures of the classroom that are manipulable to promote motivation to learn. These structures must represent the classroom organization and must relate to instructional planning.
3. Strategies need to be identified to enhance the motivation of all students, and they must be grounded in theory and research and evaluated in relation to developmental factors, other motivational constructs, and individual differences.

The following chapters in this book address the issues identified by Ames (1990). This entire book focuses on motivating students to learn. The framework used to motivate students is discussed in Chapter 3, and the specific strategies to motivate students, based on theory and research, are addressed in Chapters 4 through 7.

Summary of Main Points

- Motivation to learn is a student's tendency to find academic activities significant and worthwhile and to try to get the intended learning benefits from them.
- In some classrooms, the main goal appears to complete the worksheets and paperwork to achieve a reward or simply to move on to the next task—this is a work orientation. In other classes, instructional goals are centered on learning and understanding the material—this is a learning orientation. The learning orientation is preferred.

- Four factors characterized the teachers' practices in the classes in which students reported higher levels of motivation to learn: (a) Provide opportunities to learn, (b) press students to think, (c) support students' attempts to understand, and (d) evaluate student learning.
- Each lesson needs to be planned so that students have opportunities to learn during the lesson—bring the lesson to the student. During the lesson, students should be required to think about and use the content in some way—bring the students to the lesson.
- A comprehensive approach is needed when looking at how motivational theory and research can guide classroom practice.

Discussion/Reflective Questions

- In what ways could you alter your instruction to make it more learning oriented?
- From your experience, what are some effective ways to press students to think?
- What are some approaches that you might use to bring the lesson to the student?

Suggested Activities

- List the benefits and liabilities of a work-oriented and a learning-oriented classroom.
- Design a lesson applying the four strategies to promote learning.
- What are some factors to consider when you are planning to bring the lesson to the students and bring the students to the lesson?

3

| *A Framework for*
| *Motivating Students* |

As you no doubt can tell by now, motivating students to learn is not a simple job. The multifaceted nature of motivation requires consideration of many issues such as intrinsic and extrinsic motivation, theoretical views of motivation, and classroom learning orientations. All that information must then be considered as decisions are made about motivational strategies to use in the classroom. Furthermore, information from research and best practice indicates that a comprehensive approach to classroom decision making about motivation is the most effective.

To address these issues, the following topics are discussed in this chapter:

1. Need for a comprehensive framework
2. Some proposals for motivating students
3. The framework used in this book
4. Planning for motivation

Need for a Comprehensive Framework

To motivate students, teachers sometimes think that students just need to be praised and encouraged as a means to boost their self-image and self-confidence. But information from research and best practice suggests otherwise. Motivating students to learn is complex and multifaceted. It involves intrinsic and extrinsic motivation, along with the manipulation of a number of classroom variables such as tasks, evaluation, feedback, and expectations.

Too often, motivation involves attempts to create a work orientation with an emphasis on task completion within certain time limits and competition among students (Ames, 1992). Motivation in work-oriented classrooms often focuses on a limited number of variables affecting students' motivation to learn. In these classrooms, motivation enhancement often means using extrinsic incentives to get students to engage in certain behaviors, and motivation strategies translate into free time or special activities that are not woven into the fabric of instructional practice. Also, there may be an attempt to enhance the students' self-confidence and self-image. This can be done privately with personal goal setting and action plans.

With a learning orientation in the classroom, however, developing a plan to motivate students to learn is more complex. In doing so, the learning environment must be examined in a comprehensive way (Ames, 1992), and factors (e.g., tasks, evaluation, and authority) that can develop this learning environment must be identified. Then, a comprehensive approach to classroom intervention is needed because these factors are mutually dependent on each other and interact with each other. Therefore, a comprehensive framework is needed to motivate students to learn in a learning-oriented classroom.

Some Proposals
for Motivating Students

Some educators have organized their recommendations to motivate students around intrinsic and extrinsic motivation (e.g., Good & Brophy, 1995; Slavin, 1997). Others have provided a list of recommendations based on a synthesis of the issues (e.g., Biehler & Snowman, 1997; Gage & Berliner, 1998). Full-length books are devoted to motivating students (e.g., Brophy, 1997; McCombs & Pope, 1994; Pintrich & Schunk, 1996; Raffini, 1996; Reeve, 1996; Spaulding, 1992; Stipek, 1998).

Some authors have recognized the complexity of the motivational issues and have developed frameworks for organizing the ways to motivate students to learn. The models developed by John Keller, Raymond Wlodkowski, and Joyce Epstein are described here.

The Keller Model

Keller (1983) looked at motivating students in a comprehensive way and suggested that teachers consider four dimensions of motivation when making instruction plans: interest, relevance, expectancy, and satisfaction.

1. *Interest* is the extent to which the students' curiosity is aroused and sustained through time. Keller suggested the following approaches to stimulate and maintain students' interest and curiosity in the lesson:

- Use novel, incongruous, conflictual, and paradoxical events through an abrupt change in the status quo.
- Use anecdotes or other devices for injecting a personal, emotional element into otherwise purely intellectual or procedural material.
- Give students opportunities to learn more about things that they already know about or believe in, but also give them moderate doses of the unfamiliar and unexpected.
- Use analogies to make the strange familiar and the familiar strange.
- Guide students into a process of question generation and inquiry.

2. *Relevance* is the students' perception that instruction is related to personal needs or goals. Keller maintained that motivation increases when students perceive that a learning activity will sat-

isfy basic motives such as needs for achievement, power, or affiliation. He offered the following strategies for increasing personal relevance:

- Provide opportunities to achieve standards of excellence under conditions of moderate risk
- Make instruction responsive to the power motive by providing opportunities for choice, responsibility, and interpersonal influence
- Satisfy the need for affiliation by establishing trust and providing opportunities for no-risk, cooperative interaction

TEACHERS IN ACTION

Using Real-Life Examples for Relevance

Greg Morris, middle school science teacher,
Raleigh, North Carolina

It is essential to use a variety of teaching methods to motivate middle school students. Whenever I directly involve my students in the learning process, they come alive, and we enjoy the class. As often as possible, I use real-life examples that are meaningful to my students. Students want to know how the content connects to their lives and the "real world," and it is their right to know this.

For example, when we were studying mechanics in science class, I asked the students, "How many of you like to ride roller coasters? Why do you like to? What is your favorite roller coaster?" We recorded the results on the chalkboard and then set up a simulation of a roller coaster ride by putting pairs of chairs in a row and having students pantomime a roller coaster ride. We then viewed several video clips of people riding a roller coaster to verify our simulation. My students could not wait to come to class the next day to find out the physics behind our roller coaster ride; this made the content more relevant and meaningful.

3. *Expectancy* is the students' perceived likelihood of success through personal control. Keller offered four strategies for increasing success expectancies:

- Increase experience with success
- Be clear about the requirements for success
- Use techniques that offer personal control over success
- Provide feedback to help students relate their success to their personal effort and ability

4. *Satisfaction* refers to the students' intrinsic motivations and responses to extrinsic rewards.

- To maintain intrinsic satisfaction, provide rewards that naturally follow a task.
- To maintain intrinsic satisfaction, use unexpected, noncontingent rewards.
- To maintain intrinsic satisfaction, use verbal praise and informative feedback.
- To maintain quantity of performance, use motivating feedback following the response.
- To improve the quality of performance, provide corrective feedback when it will be immediately useful, usually just before the next opportunity to practice.

The four dimensions of the Keller model for motivating students are listed in Table 3.1.

The Wlodkowski Model

Wlodkowski (1984) noted that there are three critical periods in any learning event when particular motivational strategies will have a maximum impact on the student's motivation:

1. *Beginning a lesson*—when the student enters and starts the learning process. (Focus on attitudes and needs.)

Table 3.1 The Keller Model for Motivating Students

1. *Interest.* Refers to whether the students' curiosity is aroused and whether this arousal is sustained through time

2. *Relevance.* Refers to whether the students see the instruction as satisfying personal needs or helping achieve personal goals

3. *Expectancy.* Refers to the students' perceived likelihood of achieving success through personal control

4. *Satisfaction.* Refers to the students' intrinsic motivations and their reactions to extrinsic rewards

---

2. *During a lesson*—when the student is involved in the body or main content of the learning process. (Focus on stimulation and affect.)
3. *Ending a lesson*—when the student is finishing or completing the learning process. (Focus on competence and reinforcement.)

For each of these periods, two general motivational factors serve as categories for specific strategies. Strategies should address attitudes and needs when beginning a lesson, stimulation and affect during a lesson, and competence and reinforcement when ending a lesson. When you plan a lesson, include these motivational factors in each phase of the learning sequence.

Beginning a Lesson

At the beginning of a learning activity, you need to consider two motivational factors when selecting motivational strategies: *attitude* and *needs*. Attitude deals with the student's view of the subject matter, the general learning environment, and other factors. Needs deal with the basic needs within the student at the time of learning.

As you plan for the beginning of a learning event, ask yourself two questions:

- What can I do to establish a positive learning *attitude* for this learning sequence?
- How do I best meet the *needs* of my learners through this learning sequence?

Attitude. Attitude deals with the students' stance toward the learning environment, the teacher, subject matter, and self. When planning to incorporate motivational factors at the beginning of a lesson, you need to select strategies that positively affect the students' attitude about themselves, yourself as the teacher, the subject, and the learning situation while also establishing learner expectations for success.

To positively affect attitude about yourself as the teacher, you might plan to establish a relationship with the students by sharing something of value with them, listening to them with empathy, treating them with warmth and acceptance, and using class or individual meetings to establish relationships. To positively affect attitudes toward the subject and learning situation, plan to make conditions surrounding the subject positive, model enthusiasm for the subject taught, associate the student with other students who are enthusiastic about the subject, positively confront the student about erroneous beliefs, and make the first experience with the subject matter as positive as possible.

You can positively affect the students' attitudes toward themselves by promoting success, giving encouragement, emphasizing students' personal causation in their learning, and using group process methods to enhance a positive self-concept. Finally, when trying to establish learner expectancy for success, you could interview students and help them set goals or contracts for their learning.

Needs. A need is a condition experienced by the individual as a force that leads the person to move in the direction of a goal. Maslow's hierarchy of needs provides a useful framework to examine strategies that teachers could select in addressing students' needs at the beginning of a lesson. When planning for meeting physiological needs, select content, examples, and projects that relate to the students' physiological needs and be alert to restlessness so that you can relieve the causes producing it. For example, students may not be physically comfortable after sitting for long periods or after performing one task for a long time. Instead, have a change of activities or break the tasks up into shorter segments.

When addressing safety needs, plan to select content, examples, and projects that relate to the safety needs of students; reduce or remove components of the learning environment that lead to failure or fear; and introduce the unfamiliar through the familiar. To reduce the fear of failure, provide opportunities for practice and tell students that the practice activities will not be graded.

When planning for belongingness and love needs, select content, examples, and projects that relate to these needs; create components of the learning environment that tell students that they are wanted and cared for; and designate classroom duties and responsibilities in such a way that each student becomes a functioning member of the group. Assigning some work to be completed in groups, for example, allows opportunities for important social interaction. Careful monitoring of groups is needed, however, to respond to any negative interactions arising from cliques, bullies, or other factors.

Esteem needs can be addressed by offering learning goals that affirm the students' identities or roles; subject matter, assignments, and learning modes that appeal to and complement student strengths and assets; subject matter that enhances the students' independence as learners and as persons; and activities that allow students to publicly display and share their talents and works. For example, display composition or writing projects that require the students to incorporate information about their ethnic heritage.

To address self-actualization needs, give students the opportunity to select topics, projects, and assignments that appeal to their curiosity, sense of wonder, and need to explore; encourage divergent thinking and creativity in the learning process; and provide the opportunity for self-discovery. Community service or service learning activities, for example, can provide opportunities to meet these objectives.

During a Lesson

During a learning activity, two motivational factors need to be considered: *stimulation* and *affect*. Stimulation deals with attention and involvement during the learning process. Affect deals with the affective or emotional experience of the student while learning.

As you plan for this part of the learning activity, ask yourself two questions:

- How will this learning sequence continuously *stimulate* my learners?
- How are the *affective experience* and *emotional climate* for this learning sequence positive for learners?

Stimulation. Stimulation involves maintaining the students' attention and building involvement. When you introduce or connect learning activities, draw the students' attention to the new learning activity or topic. Use movement, voice, body language, and props to vitalize and accentuate classroom presentations. To promote interest and involvement, relate learning to student interest, and use humor, examples, analogies, stories, and questions. When asking questions, limit informational questions and selectively increase questions that require comprehension, application, analysis, synthesis, and evaluation. To create disequilibrium, introduce contrasting information, play the devil's advocate, and be unpredictable to the degree that students enjoy the spontaneity. To be unpredictable, for example, alter the way that you conduct each of the review sessions before a test as well as changing the testing format.

Affect. Affect pertains to the feelings, concerns, values, and passions of the students while learning. When planning lessons, try to encourage and integrate learner emotions, and maintain an optimal emotional climate within the learning group. Feelings are the emotions that accompany the *how* and *what* a student is learning. Awareness and communication allow feelings to become a vital and influential part of student motivation.

Integrate what is being taught with how the student feels *now* about the content and then establish a relationship between this content and the student's life. You can also take steps to establish a classroom climate that promotes positive interrelationships among class members.

Ending a Lesson

At the end of a learning activity, two motivational factors are considered: *competence* and *reinforcement*. Competence deals with the degree of progress that the students feel they have made. Reinforcement deals with feedback on their progress.

When you plan for the ending of a learning activity, ask yourself two questions:

- How does this learning sequence increase or affirm the learners' feelings of *competence?*
- What *reinforcement* does this learning sequence provide for my learners?

Competence. Competence refers to the feelings of growth and content mastery that a person recognizes. As you plan for the ending of the learning activity, take into account at least two aspects of competence. First, make sure that students have opportunities to become aware of their progress and mastery. You can do this by providing feedback on mastery of learning, offering constructive criticism, and facilitating successful completion of the learning task. Second, students need to be aware at the end of the activity that they "personally caused" their own learning. This can be done by acknowledging and affirming the students' responsibility in completing the task, using a competence checklist for student self-rating, and acknowledging the risk taking and challenge involved in the learning accomplishment.

Reinforcement. Reinforcement is an event or a state of affairs that changes subsequent behavior when it follows an instance of that behavior. For example, a student who is given praise for efforts made in studying for a test will tend to continue these efforts after the praise is given. Reinforcement can be in the form of artificial reinforcers such as tangible or concrete materials, or extrinsic symbols for learning behavior. Gold stars, prizes, trinkets, certificates, and points are examples. When natural consequences (e.g., reading

---

Table 3.2 The Wlodkowski Model for Motivating Students

---

1. *Beginning a lesson*

   When the students enter and start the learning process

   - What can I do to establish a positive learning *attitude* for this learning sequence?
   - How do I best meet the *needs* of my learners through this learning sequence?

2. *During a lesson*

   When the students are involved in the body or main content of the learning process

   - How will this learning sequence continuously *stimulate* my learners?
   - How are the *affective experience* and *emotional climate* for this learning sequence positive for learners?

3. *Ending a lesson*

   When the students are finishing or completing the learning process

   - How does this learning sequence increase or affirm the learners' feelings of *competence?*
   - What *reinforcement* does this learning sequence provide for my learners?

---

can produce new insights and expanded awareness) of student learning are evident, emphasize the result of the learning behavior and highlight it as a part of the learning process.

You can take steps to enhance the intrinsic value of traditional grading and limit its negative intrinsic value. Provide alternative forms of feedback to students about their performance, clearly explain the grading policy to students, and perhaps use student self-evaluation as part of the grading decision.

Table 3.2 reviews the Wlodkowski model for motivating students and lists the questions you should ask concerning motivational factors at the three critical periods of the learning event.

The Epstein TARGET Model

The TARGET motivational program, originally developed by Epstein (1989) for use in families, was further developed by Ames (1992) as a comprehensive approach to motivate students to learn. Epstein identified six variables that help teachers organize classroom instruction. These represent the TARGET acronym: *T*asks, *A*uthority, *R*ecognition, *G*rouping, *E*valuation, and *T*ime.

Tasks

Tasks are actions that the teacher asks students to take in an effort to have students meet the lesson objectives. Tasks are selected to provide an optimal level of challenge and to emphasize activities that students find interesting and intrinsically engaging. Students' perceptions of tasks and activities influence how they approach learning, and tasks also affect how students use available time. Because of the nature of tasks, students make judgments about their ability, their willingness to apply effortful strategies, and their feelings of satisfaction (Ames, 1992).

Tasks that involve variety and diversity are more likely to facilitate an interest in learning and a mastery orientation (e.g., Marshall & Weinstein, 1984; Nicholls, 1989). Students are also more likely to approach and engage in learning when they identify significant reasons for engaging in an activity (e.g., developing an understanding and gaining new skills; Brophy, 1987; Corno & Rohrkemper, 1985; Lepper & Hodell, 1989; Meece, 1991).

When tasks are defined with specific and short-term goals, students are more likely to believe that they can accomplish a task with reasonable effort (Schunk, 1989). As students make judgments about the tasks, they appraise the utility of planning, organizing, and monitoring strategies (Corno & Rohrkemper, 1985). The use of these self-regulatory skills is largely dependent on whether students feel enabled to manage their own learning (Paris & Winograd, 1990). When students are focused on the task or on skill improvement and value the learning, they are likely to feel empowered in their pursuits, to exhibit active engagement, and to feel more satisfied in school learning in general.

Authority

Authority in the classroom involves control over decision making concerning all aspects of instruction. Teachers, of course, have the main authority, but authority can be shared with students and exercised with consideration of their needs and feelings.

Allowing students to have a say in establishing priorities in task completion, the method of learning, or pace of learning is a way of giving responsibility to the students. Opportunities to develop self-management and self-regulatory strategies must accompany the assignment of responsibility. A positive relationship between autonomy orientation of the classroom environment and students' intrinsic motivation has been supported in numerous studies (Ames, 1992). Students' perceptions of control appear to be significant factors affecting student engagement in learning and the quality of their learning.

Students' perceptions of control have important consequences for their level of interest and engagement. In many classrooms, however, students unfortunately have few opportunities to control the selection of tasks, materials, method of learning, product, or pace.

Recognition

Recognition concerns the procedures and practices used by teachers to acknowledge students' efforts and accomplishments. Recognition is provided to all students who make noteworthy progress, not just the highest achievers.

Although recognition provides students with feedback about their performance, there are some negative effects when social comparisons are made when giving feedback. Social comparisons include announcements of the highest and lowest scores; public charts of students' papers, scores, and progress; ability grouping; and displays of selected papers and achievements.

In classrooms characterized by frequent grades and public evaluation, students become focused on their ability and the distribution of ability in the classroom group. Not only do many students come to believe that they lack ability, but also this perception becomes shared among peers (Rosenholtz & Simpson, 1984). External evaluative pressure and emphasis on social comparison information also appear to have negative consequences for students' interest (Deci & Ryan, 1985), their pursuit of challenging tasks (Elliott & Dweck, 1988), and their use of learning strategies (Ames, 1992).

As students progress through school, evaluation becomes more formal and more closely tied to performance criteria than to simple assignment completion. A negative motivational climate is created when evaluation is normative and emphasizes social comparison, is highly differentiated, and is perceived as threatening to one's sense of control (Ames, 1992). This type of evaluation undoubtedly contributes to "failure-avoiding" and "failure-accepting" patterns of achievement behavior (Covington & Omelich, 1984).

Grouping

Grouping involves the way in which students are brought together for instruction or other activities. Students may be brought together in a variety of ways—in pairs, triads, and groups of four or even more students. Grouping should be managed in ways that promote cooperative learning and minimize interpersonal competition and social comparison.

TEACHERS IN ACTION

Grouping Students for Tasks

Leslie Seff, high school English teacher,
Baltimore, Maryland

I have my 12th-grade English students work on a research paper in cooperative groups. Each student chooses a genre: science fiction, detective story, spy thriller, Gothic novel, or Victorian novel. In cooperative learning groups, the students research the characteristics and history of the genre. Then, each student in the group selects an individual novel in the chosen genre. No two students read the same novel, so each student has to find the evidence in his or her own novel to show how effective the novel was as an example of the genre. Each student later prepares a 5- to 7-page critical analysis of the novel.

As the students work through the second phase of the assignment independently, they often help each other find sources. Members of the groups often discuss the issues, helping each other reach perceptive conclusions for their papers.

Because of the groups, the students are able to prepare their research papers without giving up on the task or feeling overwhelmed. Whenever a group member runs into a snag, other students in the group are there for help. The cooperative learning groups help many fearful, insecure students accomplish this challenging task with success.

Evaluation

Evaluation involves the standards that are set by the teacher for learning and behavior, the procedures for monitoring and judging the attainment of those standards, and the methods for providing information about performance or needed improvements. Evaluation is accomplished using multiple criteria and methods, focusing on individualized assessment of progress rather than comparisons of individuals or groups.

Depending on how evaluation is structured, students may be oriented toward different goals and exhibit different patterns of motivation (Ames & Ames, 1984). For example, classrooms with a work orientation may involve more extrinsic rewards compared with classrooms with a learning orientation.

Many classrooms are highly product oriented (Brophy, 1983a, 1983b). Students are focused on the quantity of their work, and the high visibility of these products orients students away from the task of learning. This product orientation soon shifts to a work orientation when correctness, absence of errors, and normative success are emphasized.

Table 3.3 The Epstein TARGET Model for Motivating Students

---

1. *Tasks.* Actions that the teacher asks students to take in an effort to have students meet the lesson objectives

2. *Authority.* Involves control over decision making concerning all aspects of instruction

3. *Recognition.* Concerns the procedures and practices used by teachers to recognize students' efforts and accomplishments

4. *Grouping.* Involves the way in which students are brought together for instruction or other activities

5. *Evaluation.* Involves the standards that are set by the teacher for learning and behavior, the procedures for monitoring and judging the attainment of those standards, and the methods for providing information about performance or needed improvements

6. *Time.* Refers to the amount of time that is designated for learning tasks and the degree of flexibility in the use of that time

---

Time

The time that is designated for learning tasks and the degree of flexibility in the use of that time also affect students' motivation to learn. Motivation can be enhanced when time is used in creative ways that ease the constraints of rigid scheduling.

Instead of being seen as a fixed program, Epstein's TARGET model should be viewed as a framework that is adaptable to different teaching situations and useful for building motivational considerations into instructional plans. The TARGET model is summarized in Table 3.3.

The Framework Used
in This Book

The message from research and best practice is clear—develop a comprehensive approach to motivate students to learn, instead of looking at one or two classroom variables in isolation. Much of the information about motivation addresses important topics such as needs, satisfaction, authority, and recognition. Teachers, however, typically don't make planning decisions about such nebulous topics as needs and authority. Instead, teachers consider issues such as needs as they make decisions about specific areas such as tasks, evaluation approaches, and procedures for academic and behavioral expectations.

As a result, the information from research and best practice about motivating students to learn is organized in the next four chapters around decision areas that teachers consider when planning.

- Motivational Strategies Concerning Instruction (Chapter 4)
- Motivational Strategies Concerning Evaluation and Recognition (Chapter 5)
- Academic and Behavioral Expectations (Chapter 6)
- Motivating Hard-to-Reach Students (Chapter 7)

Will the strategies highlighted in this book work in all classrooms? The strategies come from research and best practice, and thus they provide a framework for classroom decisions. It is likely, however, that you will need to evaluate your own situation— grade level, subject area, and student characteristics—to determine which strategies are most appropriate in your context. Some strategies might need to be modified to work successfully in your classroom. Some strategies might be used a great deal, whereas others might not be used at all. Your professional assessment of your situation will guide your selection and use of the motivational strategies.

Planning for Motivation

When considering a comprehensive approach to motivating students in your classroom, it is important to understand the motivational concepts discussed so far. These include issues such as intrinsic and extrinsic motivation, interest, relevance, expectancy, satisfaction, needs, attitudes, stimulation, competence, authority, recognition, grouping, and evaluation.

With an understanding of these motivational issues, you then must decide how to incorporate these concepts into your instruction. Your instructional planning actually includes many time frames:

- The course
- The semester
- The marking period
- Each unit
- Each week
- Each lesson

As you consider how to incorporate the motivation concept of relevance into your instruction, for example, you would think about ways to apply that concept in each time frame listed here. How might you help students see the relevance of the entire course, and how might that be reflected in your course syllabus and introduction to the course? How might you highlight the relevance of the content during each marking period and each unit? Similarly, students would appreciate seeing the relevance of the content that is covered in each week and in each lesson.

To answer these questions, you need to think globally to help students see the big picture as well as the importance of each smaller piece of content. Your long-range planning should take the topic of relevance into account, and the relevance should be apparent in each unit and lesson. Therefore, your planning for motivation needs to be conducted for all levels of planning. Decisions need to be made about other motivational concepts as well when you conduct your planning.

TEACHERS IN ACTION

Planning for Motivation and Opportunities to Learn

Janet Roesner, elementary school mentor teacher,
Baltimore, Maryland

It is important to identify the learning goals and the indicators of learning for each unit—this provides a clear focus when planning the unit. Next, a teacher needs to determine the skills and type of thinking that the students will need to be successful in the lesson. These acquired skills then become strategies for success and can be applied to all areas of learning.

One important question to ask when planning a unit is, "How will this learning be meaningful?" Making meaningful connections to the students' background knowledge, experiences, and interests is key to motivating the learners. Giving students opportunities to decide on real-life assessments that are clearly related to the learning goals is very motivating. In this way, interest peaks, application of knowledge soars, and students succeed.

Each lesson in a unit must make meaningful connections to the learning goal. In this way, students begin to learn for understanding, rather than just for completing the work.

Summary of Main Points

- A comprehensive approach to motivate students to learn is needed because classroom factors are mutually dependent on each other and interact with each other.
- Keller highlighted four dimensions to consider when motivating students—interest, relevance, expectancy, and satisfaction.
- Wlodkowski noted three critical periods of a learning event—beginning, during, and ending—during which particular motivational strategies will have a maximum impact on the learner's motivation.

- Motivational factors to be considered include attitudes and needs at the beginning of the lesson, stimulation and affect during the lesson, and competence and reinforcement at the end of the lesson.
- Epstein identified six variables that help teachers organize classroom instruction. These variables represent the TARGET acronym: Tasks, Authority, Recognition, Grouping, Evaluation, and Time.
- Planning for motivation needs to be conducted for all levels of planning—the course, the semester, the marking period, each unit, each week, and each lesson.

Discussion/Reflective Questions

- What is the reasoning for developing a comprehensive plan for motivating students instead of using isolated strategies?
- What are the merits of the Keller, the Wlodkowski, and the Epstein models for motivating students to learn?
- Describe several ways that review can be conducted at the end of a lesson to give students a sense of competence about what they just learned.

Suggested Activities

- Select one of the motivational models reviewed in this chapter and apply those concepts to a unit that you teach.
- Select a lesson that you have taught and then decide if you need to make any changes as you apply Wlodkowski's concepts about motivational factors at the beginning, the middle, and the end of the lesson.
- Talk with other teachers to see how they plan to motivate students to learn.

Motivational Strategies Concerning Instruction

The instructional strategies that you use, the tasks that you ask students to complete, and the way in which you interact with students during instruction all influence students' motivation to learn. To address these issues, the following specific approaches are discussed in this chapter:

1. Capture student interest in the subject matter
2. Highlight the relevance of the subject matter
3. Vary instructional strategies throughout the lesson to maintain interest
4. Plan for active student involvement
5. Select strategies that capture students' curiosity
6. Select strategies and present material with an appropriate degree of challenge and difficulty
7. Group students for tasks
8. Design the lesson to promote student success
9. Allow students some control over the lessons
10. Express interest in the content, and project enthusiasm
11. Provide opportunities to learn
12. Support students' attempts to understand

Capture Student Interest in the
Subject Matter

One of the first tasks in motivating students to learn is to arouse their curiosity and sustain this interest through time (Keller, 1983). Useful techniques for capturing student interest address the inner need to know or to satisfy curiosity, thus the techniques are intrinsically satisfying. Try to incorporate the approaches described below, especially at the start of the lessons. These approaches are especially useful when introducing new material. Teachers need to model interest in the subject matter.

• *Take time to understand what students perceive as important and interesting.* To capture student interest in the subject matter, it is useful to first recognize what the students' interests are. Listen to your students. Then adapt the content and select instructional activities that address these interests.

You can identify these interests through various approaches. When you near the start of a new unit, you might briefly describe to the students what issues and activities you are currently planning. Then ask students to indicate topics or activities in which they are especially interested and to offer additional suggestions. This interaction could be in the form of an informal discussion.

You may prefer to draw a "web" of these issues on the chalkboard. To do so, write the main topic in the center of a circle; then draw lines out from the circle and write the related issue on each line. As additional lines are drawn to represent the related topics, the diagram will look like a spider's web. Still more connecting lines may be drawn. For example, a unit in health may have "first aid" written in the center of the web. Connecting lines may include topics such as burns, broken bones, shock, poisoning, calling for help, and so on. Each of these lines may have some connecting lines to provide more detail.

Another way to identify student interests is through a questionnaire about the unit topics and proposed activities. You may also devise your own ways to gather this student input. The key thing is to identify student interests in the subject matter and the possible instructional strategies and to take them into account in your planning decisions. With this information, you will be able to make better decisions to capture student attention throughout all sessions.

• *Select topics and tasks that interest students.* Whenever possible, incorporate topics that the students will find enjoyable and exciting into the lesson. Relating some current event is often a useful way to connect student interests. When considering tasks for a lesson, choose tasks that enable students to select and explore their interests in the topic while achieving the lesson objective. Students often appreciate a choice of tasks that relate to their preferred learning style.

TEACHERS IN ACTION

Capturing Student Interest Through Pen Pal Letters

Arlene Bekman, elementary school teacher mentor,
Baltimore, Maryland

When students see a need to learn the material and can apply it to a real-life situation, they are more motivated to become involved. To help develop my students' language arts skills, I arranged for them to be pen pals with students in Morocco.

Through the letter writing, the students learned how to use a friendly letter format, use descriptive language, write to a particular audience, edit and revise, research answers to questions, address an envelope, and send a letter overseas. By their third letter, it was evident that the students' writing skills had improved.

Whatever activity that is used as a vehicle to motivate students, it should be something that involves all the students and something that they see the need to learn.

- *Set the stage at the start of the lesson.* You can set the stage for learning by providing a brief, initial activity at the beginning of the lesson that is used to induce students to a state of wanting to learn. This is sometimes referred to as a *set induction*. This activity helps establish the context for the learning that is to follow and helps students engage in the learning. Set induction helps students see what the topic of the lesson is in a way that is related to their own interests and their own lives.

For example, a health lesson on the topic of first aid might begin with the reading of a newspaper report about a recent fire or accident. After reading the article, you could ask the students what they would do if they were the first ones to arrive after the accident. A number of ideas are likely to be generated in this discussion. Then you could bring that opening discussion to a close by saying that today's lesson will be about that exact topic—what type of first aid to administer for various conditions. Then you would move into the first part of the lesson. This set induction activity helps create interest in the lesson in a way that students can relate to their own lives.

Effective set induction activities should get students interested in what is to be taught during the lesson, must be connected to the content of the lesson that is to follow, must help students understand the material, and should be related to the students' lives or to a previous lesson.

- *State learning objectives and expectations at the start of the lesson.* Students need to know exactly what they are supposed to do, how they will be evaluated, and what the consequences of success will be. Avoid confusion by clearly communicating learning objectives and expectations. At the start of a class, for example, you might list the five main issues to be considered in the next unit and explain that today's lesson deals with the first issue. In this way, the students have a conceptual picture in which to organize the content.

In another example, you might describe that day's assignment, your expectations for how the assignment will be completed, the form of the paper to be turned in, the means of evaluation and relative point value in the grading period, and any other expectations you hold.

Your description of learning objectives and expectations also serves as an advance organizer for the students so they understand what will happen in class. This introduction should also include a description of the value of the subject matter to be examined and the related tasks. In this way, students can better appreciate the material and have a reason to be motivated. Advance organizers help students by focusing their attention on the subject being considered, informing them where the lesson is going, relating new material to content already understood, and providing structure for the subsequent lesson.

• *Use questions and activities to capture student interest in the subject matter.* As part of the advance organizer, or soon after the beginning of a lesson, stimulate curiosity by posing interesting questions or problems. Students will feel the need to resolve an ambiguity or obtain more information about a topic. For example, you might ask students to speculate or make predictions about what they will be learning or raise questions that successful completion of the activity will enable them to answer. Hook the students with key questions. In the study of presidents, for example, you might ask, "What are the characteristics of effective leaders?"

You may use these questions and activities as a means to induce curiosity or suspense. Divergent questions that allow several possible acceptable answers are useful (e.g., "What do you think the author was trying to express in the first eight lines of this poem?"). Provide opportunities for students to express opinions or make other responses about the subject matter.

• *Introduce the course and each topic in an interesting, informative, and challenging way.* When introducing the course and each topic, highlight the tasks to be accomplished, pique the students' interest, challenge their views, and even hint at inconsistencies to be resolved. The enthusiasm and interest in the subject that you express will carry over to the students.

Highlight the
Relevance of the Subject Matter

Another important motivational task is to help the students understand that the subject matter is related to their personal needs or goals (Keller, 1983). Actions taken to achieve this purpose can also arouse student curiosity and sustain this interest through time. You might take the following actions to highlight the relevance of the subject matter.

• *Select significant learning objectives and activities.* Students will be motivated to learn only if they see the relevance of their learning. Select academic objectives that include some knowledge or skill that is clearly worth learning, either in its own right or as a step to some greater objective. Avoid planning continued practice on skills that have already been mastered, memorizing lists for no good reason, looking up and copying definitions of terms that are never used relevantly, and other activities that do not directly relate to the learning objective.

• *Directly address the importance of each new topic examined.* Students are more likely to appreciate the relevance of the subject matter if you discuss the ways it would be useful to them, both in and out of school. They need to see the connections between the concepts and the real world. Discuss the reason why the learning objective is important—in its own right or as a step to additional, useful objectives. Relate the subject matter to today's situation and everyday life. Call students' attention to the usefulness of the knowledge and skills taught in schools to their outside lives.

Have your students think about the topics or activities in relation to their own interests. This helps students understand that motivation to learn must come from within, that it is a property of the learner, rather than a task to be learned. You might ask them, for example, to identify questions about the topic that they would like to have answered.

You might have students fill in a K-W-L Chart as an organizer for the lesson or unit to help students identify the relevance of the subject matter. The *K* is for what they *know* already about the subject. The *W* is for *what* they would like to learn about the subject. After instruction has taken place, the students could then fill in the *L*, which is for what they have *learned* about the subject matter.

• *Adapt instruction to students' knowledge, understanding, and personal experience.* The content will be more relevant to the students if you relate it to the students' personal experiences and needs and to prior knowledge. You might begin a lesson on geography by listing several state or national parks and asking students if they have visited them. You then could ask why people are interested in visiting these parks. The mountains, lakes, or other geographical features often make these parks appealing. Through this discussion, students will see the importance of the content and will more likely become actively engaged in the lesson.

TEACHERS IN ACTION

Adapting Instruction to Students' Personal Experience

Ruth Criner, first-grade teacher,
Houston, Texas

Students are motivated to write when they know the purpose of the writing or if the topic is one of their choice. I try to plan lessons around topics that interest my students, but there are times when I totally ignore my lesson plans— usually because a student or the class has brought up a topic of interest that is relevant at the time.

One day, Andrew walked in slowly. His eyes were red, and it was obvious that he had been crying. After a brief discussion with him, I learned that his mom had been rushed to the hospital the night before. "Her gallbladder was hurting." His classmates and I listened as Andrew talked about the incident. During the discussion, the students asked, "What's a gallbladder?" and "Will Andrew's mom be okay?" Andrew suggested that she might feel better if we all made get-well cards for her.

Although we usually spend the first 30 minutes of the morning writing in our journals, we spent the morning researching the gallbladder and writing get-well wishes to Andrew's mom. We used the Internet, encyclopedia, dictionary, and anatomy charts to find out more about the gallbladder. We used the information to draw pictures and write the letters.

The students were researching and writing on a topic that was relevant to them. The students put their hearts into their efforts, and at the end, Andrew had a backpack full of get-well wishes for his mom.

• *Have students use what they have previously learned.* Another way to demonstrate the relevance of the subject matter is to have students use what they have previously learned. This may be easy to do because one learning objective often provides the foundation for the next. For example, when discussing the reasons for the Civil War, you could ask the students if their earlier study of the U.S. Constitution and the Bill of Rights points to the reasons.

In this way, you reinforce the previous learning and highlight the importance of each learning objective. You demonstrate to the students that each learning objective will have some subsequent use. Whenever possible, call for previously acquired facts and concepts.

• *Illustrate the subject matter with anecdotes and concrete examples to show relevance.* Students may find little meaning in definitions, principles, or other general or abstract content unless the material can be made more concrete or visual. Promote personal identification with the content by relating experiences or telling anecdotes illustrating how the content applies to the lives of particular individuals. An initial lesson on fractions, for example, might include a discussion of how the students divide a pizza at home. This helps students see application of the content in the real world.

Vary Your Instructional Strategies Throughout the Lesson to Maintain Interest

Students often become bored if they are asked to do the same thing throughout the lesson. Student interest is maintained and even heightened if you vary your instructional approach throughout the lesson.

• *Use several instructional approaches throughout the lesson.* After capturing student interest at the start of a lesson, maintain interest by using varied approaches such as lectures, demonstrations, recitations, practice and drills, reviews, panels and debates, group projects, inquiry approaches, discovery learning and problem solving, role playing and simulation, gaming, and computer-assisted instruction. These varied approaches help link the lesson to the students' learning style preferences.

As effective as a strategy may be, students will lose interest if it is used too often or too routinely. Vary your strategies over time and try not to use the same one throughout an entire class period. Try to make sure that something about each task is new to the students, or at least different from what they have been doing. Call attention to the new element, whether it be new content, media involved, or the type of responses required.

TEACHERS IN ACTION

Using Various Instructional Strategies

Jane E. Gurnea, third-grade teacher,
Las Cruces, New Mexico

Gone are the days when a teacher could prepare a single lesson and expect to meet the needs of the majority of the students. Students in a given classroom may have a learning or communication disorder, have scotopic sensitivity, be a non-English speaker, be a visual learner, have ADD, be an auditory learner, and so on.

It is necessary to present the same concept in a variety of ways to maximize learning for all. Peer partner activities, computer software, videos, charts, guided discussions, webbing activities, and written lessons are only some of the methodologies that I use. This makes teaching a fascinating, creative career that is constantly in flux.

Becky Taylor, fourth-grade teacher,
Oregon City, Oregon

I have found that using a variety of teaching strategies keeps the students wondering what is coming next, and it also keeps me excited about the art of teaching. The students can sense that I am prepared, which shows that I place a high value on the lesson. I try to plan at least three strategies within a single lesson, contrasting the amount of student movement, the degree of independence or group work required, and the cognitive level of the content.

• *Use games, simulations, or other fun features.* Activities that students find entertaining and fun can be used to capture their attention in the subject matter. Students find these intrinsically satisfying. An instructional game is an activity in which students follow prescribed rules unlike those of reality as they strive to attain a challenging goal. Games can be used to help students learn facts and evaluate choices. Many games combine well with the drill-and-practice method of learning.

An instructional simulation re-creates or represents an actual event or situation that causes the students to act, react, and make decisions. Simulations provide a framework for using the discovery method, the inquiry approach, experiential learning, and inductive approaches to instruction. Simulations help students practice decision making, make choices, receive results, and evaluate decisions.

Games, simulations, and other activities with fun features motivate students, promote interaction, present relevant aspects of real-life situations, and make possible direct involvement in the learning process. Games and simulations are commercially available, with many now designed for use on computers. You can also devise your own games and simulations for use in the classroom.

• *Occasionally do the unexpected.* Another way to maintain student interest and to get their attention is by doing something unexpected. Note what usually goes on, and do the opposite. If you normally have a reserved presentation style, occasionally include some dramatic elements. Instead of preparing a worksheet for the class, have the students prepare it. If your discussions in social studies have been about the effects of certain events on the United States, focus your discussion on the effects on your community. An occasional departure from what the students have come to expect adds some fun and novelty to your instruction and helps maintain student interest. You might even change some of your classroom routines to add some variation.

Plan for Active Student Involvement

Rather than passively writing notes and preparing worksheets, students appreciate the opportunity to be more actively involved. As you consider ways to arrange for this student involvement, take into account the students' learning and cognitive styles.

• *Make study of the subject matter as active, investigative, adventurous, and social as possible.* Students will find the subject matter more intrinsically interesting if they are actively involved in the lesson. You can capture their interest in the lesson if the activities that you select have built-in appeal. The students' first learning experience with a new topic should incorporate these characteristics. Whenever possible, provide opportunities for students to physically move and be active.

Students might manipulate objects at their desks or move around the room for an activity. They might be allowed to investigate topics through activities that are part of an activity center or through cooperative learning tasks. Students might conduct a debate concerning a controversial issue, prepare some product as a result of a group project, or conduct a survey in the class or beyond the classroom. In addition to independent work, students need opportunities for social interaction through pairing or small groups.

TEACHERS IN ACTION

Active Student Involvement

Mike Edmondson, high school chemistry and physics teacher, Columbus, Georgia

Students learn best when they are actively involved in the learning process, so I plan a variety of ways to get students engaged in my chemistry and physics classes, including some "offbeat" activities.

I have had my classes identify and research ecological issues and then debate them in front of audiences and even write editorials for the local newspaper. My chemistry students have designed a mural-sized periodic table and various wall murals on other topics. They have used computer software to study the content, designed crossword puzzles about course content, written essays for science contests, and even participated in a cooking contest in which students designed and cooked their own recipes and then related the processes to chemistry.

My physics students have used toys to explain physical principles, built kites to study aerodynamics, and designed and built mobiles based on physics principles. We visited a large community theater to study how pulleys and counterweights are used to move sets and scenery. After reading about quantum theory, students presented skits in groups to illustrate the fundamental principles. We have used electric trains to determine velocity and acceleration, and we include art and music in the design of many projects. In addition, the students have served as tutors in elementary classrooms.

• *Vary the type of involvement when considering the students'*
learning and cognitive styles. Information about multiple intelligences
and brain hemisphericity can be used to plan various types of student involvement. Gardner (1985) believes that all people have
multiple intelligences. He identified seven independent intelligences—
linguistic, musical, logical-mathematical, spatial, bodily kinesthetic,
interpersonal, and intrapersonal. To address the various intelligences of your students, plan for some activities that involve movement, student discussion, outlining, charting, organizing, and so
on. A number of good sources are available offering suggestions for
ways to incorporate the multiple intelligences into your teaching
(e.g., Campbell, Campbell, & Dickinson, 1999; Chapman, 1993;
Fogarty, 1997; Lazear, 1991).

Brain hemisphericity is another aspect to consider when planning for student involvement. Research on the human brain indicates that there are hemisphere-specific skills. The left side of the
brain helps people be more analytical in their orientation and deal
with facts in a logical, concrete, and sequential manner. The right
side of the brain helps people be more holistic in their thinking and
use their visual and spatial skills when learning. As you plan for
student involvement, incorporate tasks that require skills from
both sides of the brain in an effort to maintain student interest and
involvement.

Recognize that students' learning and cognitive styles determine their level of comfort and challenge in learning tasks. Students need times when they are comfortable with the tasks but also
times when they are challenged by strategies outside their preferred learning or cognitive styles. You might allow students to
choose from a menu of activities, for example, but also have them
complete certain activities.

Select Strategies
That Capture Students' Curiosity

If students are curious about the content, they are more likely to
be interested in participating in the lesson. You can capture students' curiosity in various ways outlined here.

• *Select tasks that capitalize on the arousal value of suspense, discovery, curiosity, exploration, and fantasy.* Stimuli that are novel, surprising, complex, incongruous, or ambiguous help lead to cognitive arousal. When their curiosity is aroused, students are motivated to find ways to understand the novel stimulus. This is especially important at the start of a learning experience where you are trying to capture students' attention.

Curiosity can be aroused through (a) surprise; (b) doubt, or conflict between belief and disbelief; (c) perplexity, or uncertainty; (d) bafflement, or facing conflicting demands; (e) contradiction; and (f) fantasy (Lepper & Hodell, 1989). With these strategies, a conceptual conflict is aroused. The motivation lasts until the conflict is resolved or until the students give up. If they cannot resolve the conflict, they will become bored or frustrated, so the activity should lead to resolution of the conflict to capture and maintain student interest.

Let's look at some examples of how these strategies might be used.

1. *Surprise* could result when an activity leads to an unexpected ending; for example, a ball passes through a metal ring when cold but cannot pass through after being heated.
2. *Doubt* could be created when students are asked if the interior angles of a triangle always total 180 degrees.
3. *Perplexity or uncertainty* could be created when a number of possible solutions to an issue are available, but none seems absolutely right. Creative problem-solving activities can address issues of uncertainty.
4. *Bafflement* occurs when there does not seem to be a reasonable solution to an issue.
5. *Contradiction* occurs when the solution is opposite of a general principle or common sense. Contradiction can be introduced in science with the use of discrepant events, such as a long needle being pushed through a balloon and the balloon not breaking.
6. *Fantasy* can be created by using an imaginary situation as the context for the activity. In a writing activity, for example, you might turn the lights out in the room, describe a

cave that the students might be exploring, and then have the students write a creative story about their imagined trip in the cave.

TEACHERS IN ACTION

Hooking Students on Confusion

Nancy Nega, middle school science teacher,
Elmhurst, Illinois

One of the best ways to interest students in a topic is to introduce the topic in a way that confuses or astounds them. Using a demonstration of a discrepant event is sure to capture and hold student interest. Making the demonstration interactive and involving as many students as possible increase the chances of success.

For example, when introducing the idea of air pressure, I use a 2-liter plastic bottle. I pour a small amount of very warm water into it, swirl it around, pour it out, and immediately cap the bottle. I set the bottle where the whole class can see it and then continue talking. Within a few minutes, the class notices that the bottle has started to cave in. I have them write in their notebooks what they observe and what they think is causing it. Soon, the bottle is completely caved in. They are in awe of what they see and can understand the idea of a higher pressure being "stronger" than a lower pressure. Demonstrations such as this make an impression on the students, raise their curiosity, and start the investigation of a topic in a positive, interesting, and challenging way.

• *Use anecdotes or other devices to include a personal, emotional element in the content.* When students feel that they have some personal or emotional connection to the content, their curiosity and interest will be enhanced. Therefore, try to link the content to students' emotions and personal experiences whenever possible. When examining civil rights, for example, you might ask your students if they have experienced any situation in which they have been treated unfairly because of gender, ethnicity, or other factor. In this way, students have an emotional connection to the content.

Select Strategies and Present Material With an Appropriate Degree of Challenge and Difficulty

Students are motivated when the learning tasks are challenging and interesting. You should monitor the difficulty of the learning tasks, break down difficult tasks into smaller parts, and select higher-level outcomes whenever possible.

• *Assign moderately difficult tasks that can be completed with reasonable effort.* Students lose interest rapidly if they are not able to succeed because the work is too hard or if they are able to succeed too easily when the work is not challenging enough. Activities should be at a moderate level of difficulty to maintain student interest and involvement.

Assessments conducted before instruction determine what your students already know and thus help you decide on the appropriate degree of difficulty for the work at hand. Also, carefully observe students at work to see if there is an appropriate level of difficulty.

You might provide students with a menu of tasks to be completed in a unit: Some tasks might be required, and some may be optional. The optional list should include some moderately difficult and some challenging tasks, allowing students to choose those that are moderately challenging to them.

• *Divide difficult tasks into smaller parts that are achievable without requiring excessive effort.* When difficult content or tasks are scheduled, break the activities down into smaller parts so that each part is challenging yet manageable for students to complete. Once each part is completed, the students can look back with pride at their accomplishments with difficult content.

• *Focus on higher-order learning outcomes.* Higher-level outcomes are often more intrinsically challenging and interesting to students. The lower levels of the cognitive domain include knowledge, comprehension, and application. Important curricular content is addressed at those levels.

The higher levels of the cognitive domain include analysis, synthesis, and evaluation. These levels require students to do something with the knowledge—to differentiate, relate, categorize, explain, reorganize, appraise, compare, justify, and so on. These higher-level outcomes often involve a higher level of difficulty and require students to be engaged in a variety of learning activities that are seen as interesting and challenging.

• *Monitor the level of difficulty of assignments and tests.* Students' expectations for success erode quickly when teachers repeatedly give assignments and tests that are very difficult. Continuously check to see that your assignments and tests are at a reasonable level of difficulty and that students have a good opportunity to be successful. Also, help your students learn from their errors. You could retest students until they reach mastery.

Group Students for Tasks

Arranging for various ways to group students can have a positive effect on student motivation. Grouping students promotes cooperation and teamwork.

• *Plan to use a variety of individual, cooperative, and competitive activities.* The way that you group students will be affected by the types of activities you want your students to complete. Interest is maintained when there is variety in the way the learning activities are structured. Some activities, such as seatwork, may be completed individually. Other projects can be completed in cooperative learning groups with four to six students in each group.

Competitive activities also can be used to provide excitement and rewards. Students can compete either as individuals or as teams, depending on the game or competition used. Team approaches may be more desirable because they can be structured so that students cooperate with members of their team. Make use of group competitive situations that stress fun, rather than winning.

• *Promote cooperation and teamwork.* To satisfy students' needs for affiliation, provide opportunities for no-risk, cooperative interaction. As you form groups, take into account such factors as the size of the group, the ability of group members, and gender and ethnic composition. Cooperative learning activities enable students to work together, thus minimizing individual fears of failure and competition among students. Each student in a group, however, must be held accountable for his or her contribution to the group. This could be achieved by participation points or other approaches.

TEACHERS IN ACTION

Grouping Students in a Jigsaw Activity

*Alicia Ruppersberger, middle school teacher,
Towson, Maryland*

I like to use student-centered activities that actively engage students in the learning process. One type of strategy is the jigsaw (Aronson & Patnoe, 1997). In this activity, students are assigned to groups and given individual and group assignments. They work independently or with members from other teams to share and teach the new knowledge with their teammates. I am able to assess the students by observing whether the students are using knowledge in a meaningful way, staying on task, and/or using critical or creative thinking skills and strategies. Cooperation, organization, and communication skills can also be observed.

Design the Lesson to
Promote Student Success

Motivation to learn is enhanced when students are interested in the subject matter and expect to be successful (Keller, 1983). The lesson should be designed to accomplish these ends. The following techniques are intended to achieve these purposes through both intrinsic and extrinsic motivation.

• *Design activities that lead to student success.* Students are motivated to learn when they expect to be successful. Therefore, make sure that they fairly consistently achieve success at their early level of understanding, then help them move ahead in small steps, preparing them for each step so that they can adjust to the new step without confusion or frustration. Pace students through activities as briskly as possible while thoroughly preparing them for new activities.

• *Adapt the tasks to match the motivational needs of the students.* Individual differences in ability, background, and attitudes toward school and specific subjects should be considered as you make decisions about motivational strategies. Some students need more structure than others. Other students need more reinforcement and praise. Some students are more motivated to learn than others. You will need to select motivational strategies that are most effective for your students and adjust the frequency and intensity of their use depending on individual needs.

• *Communicate desirable expectations and attributes.* If you treat your students as if they already are eager learners, they are more likely to become eager learners. Let them know that you expect them to be curious, to want to learn facts and understand principles, to master skills, and to recognize what they are learning as significant and applicable to their everyday lives. Encourage questions and inquiry. Through these means, you communicate desirable expectations and attributes.

• *Establish a supportive environment.* Be encouraging and patient in an effort to make students comfortable about learning activities and to support their learning efforts. Establish a businesslike yet relaxed and supportive classroom atmosphere. Reinforce students' involvement with the subject matter and eliminate any unpleasant consequences. Organize and manage your classroom to establish an effective learning environment.

• *Use familiar material for initial examples, but provide unique and unexpected contexts when applying concepts and principles.* When you want to build interest, involve the familiar. For applications once learning has been achieved, however, unique and unexpected examples keep interest high and help students transfer what they have learned. For example, when teaching students about the classification system for plants and animals, you might begin by classifying different types of dogs to illustrate classification. You could then have them develop a classification system for music sold on compact discs and cassette tapes at a local music store.

• *Minimize performance anxiety.* To be motivated to learn, students need to believe that they will be successful in their efforts. If you establish situations that cause tension, pressure, and anxiety, your students will likely choose safety and remain uninvolved for fear of failure. On the other hand, if you minimize risks and make learning seem exciting and worthwhile, most students will join in.

One way to reduce anxiety is to make clear the separations between instruction or practice activities designed to promote learning and tests designed to evaluate student performance. Most classroom activities should be structured as learning experiences, rather than tests. You might say, for example, "Let's assess our progress and learn from our mistakes."

To encourage participation, make it clear that students will not be graded on their questions or comments during recitation. Don't impose conditions or restrictions on assignments, homework, or projects that might get in the way of students giving their whole effort. For example, requiring all papers to be typed perfectly with no typing or formatting errors may seem to be a barrier to some students.

TEACHERS IN ACTION

Appointment Clocks for No-Risk Cooperation

Deleen Baker, K-6 reading specialist,
Oregon City, Oregon

I find that compared with primary grade students, intermediate grade students are less likely to share their knowledge and learning with peers because of concerns about being ridiculed if they make errors. As a result, I have used "Appointment Clocks" as a means to group students for no-risk cooperation in learning activities.

Before a lesson begins, I direct all students to draw a clock and to place the times for 12, 3, 6, and 9 on their clock. After setting the scene for the lesson, students are instructed to move quietly around the room and make appointments with four students (one at each of the times they placed on their clock) and to record on their clock sheet what their appointment hopes to learn in the lesson that is to follow.

After the lesson is presented, I use the Appointment Clock as a way to check for understanding. I ask the students to meet with their 6:00 appointment, for example, to compare two characters in a poem we just read, to list the three main points in the lesson, or to do some task designed to summarize and analyze the lesson.

Even students who are shy to speak in front of the class work well with the Appointment Clock sessions. Those who are reluctant learners are motivated to listen and complete the tasks assigned so that they can successfully contribute to the meetings.

Danielle is a very shy and reserved student who has difficulty expressing her thoughts in front of a group. With the Appointment Clock, she has gained confidence and feels that she is helping her partners. I have also found this approach to be effective in working with English-as-second-language students. Through Appointment Clocks, students are motivated to learn and work cooperatively, and I receive the assessment of student understanding.

Allow Students Some Control Over the Lessons

Allowing students some control over the lessons helps them develop responsibility and independence. It also provides students with opportunities to develop self-management skills and to feel as if they have some authority in the instructional situation. To the extent possible, allow students choices concerning instruction, but be sure to monitor their choices so that the students are still able to be successful.

• *Promote feelings of control by allowing students a voice in decision making.* To the extent possible, allow students a degree of control over their learning. Students who feel they can control the situation for learning (where, when, and how) and the outcomes for learning (seeking the level they want to achieve) are more intrinsically motivated (Lepper & Hodell, 1989). This will help students feel that they can be successful in their learning.

Depending on your situation, the range of choices that you give students may be limited or broad. The degree of control you permit will be affected by the students' age and maturity, among other factors. Students appreciate even a limited degree of choice. For example, you might let students select the instructional activities from a menu of choices, the order in which they must be completed, when they are due, and how they should be completed. Then, students are more likely to have expectations for success.

• *Monitor the difficulty of the goals and tasks that students choose for themselves.* When choices are available, students should be counseled to select moderately difficult goals that they can reasonably expect to achieve. If they do not establish suitable goals, you can help them determine what to do to achieve such goals. When you include help sessions, study sheets, review sessions, or even training on study skills, students are more likely to feel that even moderately difficult goals can be achieved.

There may be times when you need to prepare a contract to address the learning needs of individual students. The parents, the student, and possibly others may be involved in the preparation of this learning contract. Even in these cases, it is important to monitor the difficulty of the goals and tasks and to make adjustments as the need warrants.

Express Interest in the Content, and Project Enthusiasm

To be motivated to learn, students need to be interested in the subject matter and see its relevance (Keller, 1983). By expressing interest in the content yourself and projecting enthusiasm, you address these motivational issues.

• *Model interest and enthusiasm in the topic and in learning.* Let your students see that you value learning as a rewarding, self-actualizing activity that produces personal satisfaction and enriches your life. Furthermore, share your thinking about learning and provide examples for its application. In this way, students see how an educated person uses information in everyday life. For example, a social studies teacher might relate how her understanding of community, state, and national events helped her make informed decisions when voting on candidates during political elections. If you display a scholarly attitude while teaching and seem genuinely interested in achieving understanding, then your students are more likely to display these values.

• *Project enthusiasm.* Everything that you say should communicate in both tone and manner that the subject matter is important. If you model appropriate attitudes and beliefs about topics and assignments, the students will pick up on these cues. Use timing, nonverbal expressions and gestures, and cuing and other verbal techniques to project a level of intensity and enthusiasm that tells the students that the material is important and deserves close attention.

• *Introduce tasks in a positive, enthusiastic manner.* It is especially important to be positive and enthusiastic when introducing tasks that you expect students to complete. Introducing new tasks involves actions such as providing clear directions, discussing the importance of the material, going over examples, and responding to student questions. Your positive manner will likely affect the attitude your students carry as they complete the tasks.

• *Expect interest, not boredom, from the students.* If you think that the students will find the material boring, then students typically react with indifference and boredom. If you treat students as active, motivated learners who care about their learning and who are trying to understand, however, then positive motivation is much more likely to occur. Students will typically rise to the expectations of their instructor.

Provide Opportunities to Learn

Higher levels of student motivation to learn occur in classrooms in which teachers not only go over the material but also take specific actions to provide students with opportunities to learn (Blumenfeld et al., 1992). These actions include the following:

- *Focus lessons around midlevel concepts that are substantive but not overwhelming to students.* Midlevel concepts are likely to be challenging but achievable. New material is presented, and most students should be able to successfully learn it.
- *Make the main ideas evident in presentations, demonstrations, discussions, and assignments.* Obscure facts and insignificant information are not emphasized. Instead, make the main concepts apparent in every aspect of the lesson—in the introduction at the start of the lesson, the notes and instructional materials, the assignments, and the evaluation.
- *Present concrete illustrations of the content, and relate unfamiliar information to your students' personal knowledge.* When new content is introduced, specific examples should be provided to enhance student learning. Especially in cases in which students may be totally unfamiliar with the content, it is useful to relate the content to some aspect of the students' personal experiences. For example, when considering the types of cadence in several lines of poetry, you might provide an example of the cadence in a popular song familiar to the students.
- *Make explicit connections between new information and content that students have learned previously, and point out relationships among new ideas by stressing similarities and differences.* By deliberately referring to related content previously covered, you repeat and reinforce some of the content, which will enhance understanding. You also can show how the content previously covered and the new content are connected. In a U.S. history class, for example, you might refer back to the causes of World War I when examining the causes of World War II. In doing so, you can show any similarities and differences. Students are likely to leave with a better understanding of both wars.
- *Elaborate extensively on textbook readings, rather than allowing the book to carry the lesson.* By supplementing the textbook, you can bring in contemporary information, real-life examples, and unique extra resources that enrich your students' understanding of the textbook content. Furthermore, your elaborations and supplements make the class more interesting to the students.

• *Guide students' thinking when posing high-level questions.* High-level questions may require students to analyze, synthesize, and evaluate the content in some significant way, and some students may have difficulty with this. You may need to guide your students' thinking by carefully sequencing the questions so that the students are better able to answer correctly. Or, you may need to provide clues or some type of assistance when dealing with high-level questions.

• *Ask students to summarize, make comparisons between related concepts, and apply the information they are learning.* After students learn new content, it is important to provide an opportunity for the students to summarize and process their learning in some way before moving ahead with new material. This summary helps students organize their learning and demonstrate their understanding. Advance organizers used earlier in the lesson may help students understand the concepts and apply the information.

Support Students' Attempts to Understand

Higher levels of student motivation to learn occur in classrooms in which teachers take extra steps to support students' attempts to understand the material (Blumenfeld et al., 1992). These actions include the following:

• *Model thinking and problem solving, and work with students to solve problems when the students have difficulty.* Instead of just providing the correct answers, make deliberate efforts to help students understand. You might describe how you organize and remember the content in *your* mind. You might suggest various types of memory strategies for the students. When students have difficulty, guide them through the problem so that they will know how to deal with it the next time. You could think "out loud" as you demonstrate to students how they might approach an issue or problem.

Modeling opportunities arise whenever an academic activity calls for use of some cognitive process or strategy. For example, you can model for them how to conduct an experiment, identify the main ideas in paragraphs, develop a plan for writing a composition, or deduce applications of a general principle to specific situations.

- *Keep the procedures in instructional tasks simple.* Sometimes, the procedures used in instructional tasks get in the way of student learning. To overcome this problem, keep the procedures as simple as possible. To help students with the procedures, you could demonstrate the procedures, highlight problems, provide examples, and allow for sufficient time for work completion.
- *Encourage collaborative efforts by requiring all students to make contributions to the group.* Students may better understand the content when interacting with other students in some way about the content. Provide opportunities for students to work together to share and process the content.

Table 4.1 provides a summary of the specific approaches involved in the 12 categories of motivational strategies concerning instruction.

Summary of Main Points

- The instructional strategies that you use, the tasks that you ask students to complete, and the way in which you interact with students during instruction all influence students' motivation to learn.
- Specific approaches concerning motivational strategies for instruction are outlined in Table 4.1.

Discussion/Reflective Questions

- What are some factors to consider when determining the degree of control you will give your students in decision making about content, activities, and assignments?
- What are the merits and disadvantages of offering students choices in instructional tasks and requirements?
- How do parents affect the success of your classroom's motivational strategies?

Table 4.1 Motivational Strategies Concerning Instruction

1. *Capture Student Interest in the Subject Matter*
   a. Take time to understand what students perceive as important and interesting.
   b. Select topics and tasks that interest students.
   c. Set the stage at the start of the lesson.
   d. State learning objectives and expectations at the start of the lesson.
   e. Use questions and activities to capture student interest in the subject matter.
   f. Introduce the course and each topic in an interesting, informative, and challenging way.

2. *Highlight the Relevance of the Subject Matter*
   a. Select significant learning objectives and activities.
   b. Directly address the importance of each new topic examined.
   c. Adapt instruction to students' knowledge, understanding, and personal experience.
   d. Have students use what they have previously learned.
   e. Illustrate the subject matter with anecdotes and concrete examples to show relevance.

3. *Vary Your Instructional Strategies Throughout the Lesson to Maintain Interest*
   a. Use several instructional approaches throughout the lesson.
   b. Use games, simulations, or other fun features.
   c. Occasionally do the unexpected.

4. *Plan for Active Student Involvement*
   a. Make study of the subject matter as active, investigative, adventurous, and social as possible.
   b. Vary the type of involvement when considering the students' learning and cognitive styles.

5. *Select Strategies That Capture Students' Curiosity*
   a. Capitalize on the arousal value of suspense, discovery, curiosity, exploration, and fantasy.
   b. Use anecdotes or other devices to include a personal, emotional element in the content.

Table 4.1 (Continued)

6. *Select Strategies and Present Material With an Appropriate Degree of Challenge and Difficulty*
   a. Assign moderately difficult tasks that can be completed with reasonable effort.
   b. Divide difficult tasks into smaller parts that are achievable without requiring excessive effort.
   c. Focus on higher-order learning outcomes.
   d. Monitor the level of difficulty of assignments and tests.

7. *Group Students for Tasks*
   a. Plan to use a variety of individual, cooperative, and competitive activities.
   b. Promote cooperation and teamwork.

8. *Design the Lesson to Promote Student Success*
   a. Design activities that lead to student success.
   b. Adapt the tasks to match the motivational needs of the students.
   c. Communicate desirable expectations and attributes.
   d. Establish a supportive environment.
   e. Use familiar material for initial examples, but provide unique and unexpected contexts when applying concepts and principles.
   f. Minimize performance anxiety.

9. *Allow Students Some Control Over the Lessons*
   a. Promote feelings of control by allowing students a voice in decision making.
   b. Monitor the difficulty of the goals and tasks that students choose for themselves.

10. *Express Interest in the Content, and Project Enthusiasm*
    a. Model interest and enthusiasm in the topic and in learning.
    b. Project enthusiasm.
    c. Introduce tasks in a positive, enthusiastic manner.
    d. Expect interest, not boredom, from the students.

(Continued)

Table 4.1 (Continued)

11. *Provide Opportunities to Learn*
    a. Focus lessons around midlevel concepts that are substantive but not overwhelming to students.
    b. Make the main ideas evident in presentations, demonstrations, discussions, and assignments.
    c. Present concrete illustrations of the content and relate unfamiliar information to your students' personal knowledge.
    d. Make explicit connections between new information and content that students have learned previously, and point out relationships among new ideas by stressing similarities and differences.
    e. Elaborate extensively on textbook readings, rather than allowing the book to carry the lesson.
    f. Guide students' thinking when posing high-level questions.
    g. Ask students to summarize, make comparisons between related concepts, and apply the information they are learning.

12. *Support Students' Attempts to Understand*
    a. Model thinking and problem solving, and work with students to solve problems when they have difficulty.
    b. Keep the procedures in instructional tasks simple.
    c. Encourage collaborative efforts by requiring all students to make contributions to the group.

Suggested Activities

- Examine lesson plans that you previously prepared and critique them in relation to the 12 categories of suggested strategies in this chapter.
- Design a lesson introducing multiplication (or a topic that you teach) that honors a variety of learners.
- Talk with other teachers at your grade level or in your subject area to see how they apply the 12 categories of suggested strategies in this chapter.

5

Motivational Strategies Concerning Evaluation and Recognition

The way that you evaluate student performance and provide recognition influences students' motivation to learn. To address these issues, the following specific approaches are discussed in this chapter:

1. Establish evaluation expectations and criteria
2. Select procedures for monitoring and judging
3. Decide when to give feedback and rewards
4. Select the types of feedback and rewards
5. Help students feel satisfied with their learning outcomes
6. Use mistakes and redoing work as learning opportunities
7. Press students to think

Establish Evaluation Expectations and Criteria

Student learning can be fostered when the evaluation expectations and criteria are consistent with motivational principles (Ames, 1992; Blumenfeld et al., 1992; Stipek, 1996, 1998). The evaluation and reward system should focus on effort, improvement, and mastery. Factors that students have control over should be emphasized, and competition should be minimized.

• *Develop an evaluation system that focuses on effort, individual improvement, and mastery, rather than on work completion, getting the right answer, and comparisons with others.* In an evaluation with these focal points, learning goals will be fostered, and student attention will be directed to their own achievement.

TEACHERS IN ACTION

Using Rubrics for Assessment

Jane E. Gurnea, third-grade teacher,
Las Cruces, New Mexico

Students can best meet expectations that are clearly stated and outlined. Rubrics can be used to present minimum and maximum expectations so that students can meet performance standards. Regardless of language or special education needs, my third graders perform at higher levels when rubrics are used. These same students then participate in self-evaluation by applying the rubrics to their products. I design the steps in the rubrics to include the expected learning outcomes, and I am continually amazed at the actual learning my students achieve.

Here is an example of a language arts rubric that I have used in my classroom:

# of Points	Sentences	Spelling and Punctuation
Maximum	8+ complete sentences	Correct spelling/ correct punctuation
Average	5 complete sentences	Mostly correct spelling/ punctuation
Minimum	3 sentences	Little correct spelling/ no punctuation

• *Make rewards contingent on effort, improvement, and good performance.* If your evaluation system focuses on effort, improvement, and good performance, then any rewards provided students should be contingent on those same features. Recognize that there is a range of ability levels in the classroom and that all students should be expected to demonstrate good performance for their ability, even high-ability students.

• *Avoid norm-referenced grading systems.* When teachers grade on a curve, they ensure that some students will have a failing grade. This grading system reinforces negative expectations, promotes competition among students, and limits the number of students who receive positive reinforcement. Criterion-referenced grading systems are preferred.

• *Describe evaluations as feedback to show how well students are doing.* For consistency with the focus of your evaluation system, students need to see that feedback given to them will serve as feedback on their performance. Any feedback needs to be balanced, specific, and given in a timely way. Some teachers use a three-to-one rule—three positive statements to one negative statement when giving feedback.

• *Emphasize the factors that students have control over as affecting their performance.* Factors that students have control over include effort, note taking, persistence, preparation, and other issues. Minimize reference to uncontrollable factors such as mood, luck, ease or difficulty of the unit, and poor test items.

• *Minimize the use of competition and comparisons with others when evaluating students.* Competition can be used to prompt students to apply more effort, but it has drawbacks. Competition focuses students' attention on winning, often at the expense of valuing the new content being addressed. Failure in a competitive situation also undermines self-esteem and prompts students to blame their failure on lack of ability, rather than on lack of effort. To avoid these difficulties, minimize your use of competition and stress the cooperative nature of learning.

• *If competition is used, make sure all students have an equal chance of "winning."* Don't use the highest score as the only criterion when determining the winner in any classroom competition. Depending on the activity, your winning criterion might focus on the most creative, most unusual, most perceptive, most decorative, or a host of other possibilities.

• *Avoid unnecessary differential treatment of high and low achievers.* Criteria and feedback to students should be consistent whether the students are high or low achievers. Teachers sometimes expect less of low achievers and then provide positive statements when their performance is not necessarily praiseworthy.

Select Procedures for Monitoring and Judging

Student motivation to learn can be enhanced by taking intrinsic motivation and learning goals into account when selecting procedures for monitoring and judging student performance (Ames, 1992; Stipek, 1998). To be satisfied with their work, students need to receive feedback about their progress.

• *Use several approaches to evaluation to give students information about their accomplishments.* Rather than relying on one means of evaluating students, use several approaches to provide students information about their performance. Tests, homework, projects, drill and practice, recitation, boardwork, and seatwork often measure different types of knowledge and skills. Multiple approaches provide students with a broader base of information, in addition to providing several means for students to demonstrate their knowledge and skills.

In addition, active response opportunities can occur through projects, experiments, role plays, simulations, and other creative applications of what has been learned. Students also like activities that allow them to create a finished product. All these activities offer opportunities for students to work with and respond to instructional stimuli, and they give you opportunities to provide feedback about the students' work.

• *Provide frequent opportunities for students to respond to and to receive feedback about their academic work.* Frequent feedback is needed throughout the grading period to provide students with reinforcement about their successes and to indicate areas that need improvement. This helps students feel satisfied about their work, and it can be a tool to fuel extra effort and commitment in the event of dissatisfaction.

Give many short tests rather than a few major tests. This provides students more opportunities to correct poor performance. Students should realize that a single poor performance will not do irreversible damage to their grades. Preparing for a short evaluation is also more manageable for students. Because students need frequent feedback, plan to use several evaluation approaches for students to demonstrate their competence.

• *Provide immediate feedback about student performance whenever possible.* Students also need to receive immediate feedback that can be used to guide subsequent responses. Drill, recitation, boardwork, and seatwork can be used to provide immediate feedback. For example, you might have five students at a time work on math problems at the chalkboard while you and the rest of the class watch them. You could then offer the students feedback about their work and discuss how to overcome the difficulties they had in arriving at a solution. Students profit from this feedback, which guides them in solving future problems.

TEACHERS IN ACTION
Giving Immediate Feedback With a Stamp

Leslie Seff, high school English teacher,
Baltimore, Maryland

Many high school teachers underestimate the value of simple, external reinforcing techniques. I use a Koala Bear stamp to encourage correctness, on-task behavior, and excellence. In our study of *Macbeth,* for example, we worked on paraphrasing skills. At the end of Act III, I wanted students to make a connection between the animal imagery in the play and the plot. The students were asked to paraphrase two quotes with snake images. As they worked, I circulated around the room with the stamp. I defined the criteria for the stamp in this case as a precise, accurate paraphrase.

I gave students feedback by pointing out parts of the paraphrase that were not quite on the mark, and students had to go back and rework their answers. Eventually, I gave a limited number of stamps to the most accurate answers. Everyone in the class who completed the assignment on time and with correct answers on their papers would get full credit. Koala Bear stamps were used in this case as bonus points. Everyone wants to be recognized for a good job, and immediate recognition such as that given with the Koala Bear stamp is a powerful tool in inspiring students to make the extra effort.

• *Limit practices that focus students' attention on extrinsic reasons for engaging in tasks* (e.g., close monitoring, deadlines, threats of punishment, and competition). Although it may be necessary to closely monitor student progress and have deadlines, students' attention should be directed to their own progress and mastery of the content, rather than to the extrinsic reasons for completing the tasks.

• *Make evaluation private, not public.* Evaluation information is personal and should be given privately to the student. If this information were made public, students would feel that it is a competitive situation, which you do not want to emphasize.

Decide When to
Give Feedback and Rewards

Students need to reach a point of satisfaction with what they are doing and what they are achieving (Keller, 1983). This satisfaction is the result of their intrinsic motivations about what they are doing as well as their responses to extrinsic rewards. You can help students be satisfied by providing feedback and rewards for their performance.

- *Give some rewards early in the learning experience.* If you provide some type of reward early in the learning experience, students will likely put forth more effort to receive additional rewards. The reward may simply be praise or an opportunity for a special activity. Ultimately, students will feel satisfied, which is a motivator to learn.

Select easy tasks in the early steps of the learning activity. This offers you opportunities to deliver praise and rewards, which in turn help influence subsequent student behavior. Every student should be able to receive some type of positive reinforcement early in the lesson. For example, you might select fairly simple sentence translations in the first part of a French class but then gradually lead to more difficult translations later in the class. This gives you an opportunity to reward and reinforce students at an early point.

- *Use motivating feedback following correct responses to maintain the quantity of student performance.* Students need to receive the satisfaction of receiving recognition for their successful performance. This extrinsically reinforces students for their actions. Students are then more likely to continue performing the instructional tasks.
- *Provide corrective feedback when it will be immediately useful to improve the quality of performance.* This corrective feedback can be given just before the next opportunity to practice. In this way, students receive feedback before they are expected to perform the next activity. If students had been making errors in math class, for example, you could give corrective suggestions to students just before they begin working on sample problems in class.

Select the
Types of Feedback and Rewards

Feedback and rewards for students can come in various forms. Praise, informative feedback, and rewards are satisfying to students and can affect the quantity and quality of student performance.

- *Use verbal praise and informative feedback.* Intrinsic satisfaction with instruction can be enhanced with verbal praise and other types of informative feedback, rather than threats or close monitoring. In this way, students feel satisfaction with the progress they have made. Too much verbal praise, however, may become ineffective. Specific praise statements should focus on the students' behavior.
- *Offer rewards as incentives but only when necessary.* Rewards motivate many students to put forth effort, especially if they are offered in advance as incentives for reaching a certain level of performance. To ensure that rewards act as incentives for everyone and not just for those of high ability, see that all students have reasonable opportunities to receive rewards.

When students receive consequences that they value, they become satisfied with themselves. This helps motivate students to continue working in ways that lead to success. Rewards can be delivered in various ways, including (a) grades; (b) spoken and written praise; (c) activity rewards and special privileges (opportunities to play games, use special equipment, or engage in special activities); (d) symbolic rewards (honor roll and posting good papers); (e) material rewards (prizes and trinkets); and (f) teacher rewards (opportunities to do things with the teacher). As was discussed previously, be cautious about relying too heavily on extrinsic rewards because this may become counterproductive.

- *Make rewards contingent on mastery or a performance level that each student can achieve with effort.* Through this approach, students receive positive information about competence, and it is intrinsically satisfying that they reached the mastery level.
- *Provide substantive, informative evaluation that is based on mastery, rather than on social norms.* Feedback about performance is intrinsically satisfying for students. In contrast, feedback about how the student performed in relation to other students may promote feelings of competition, which is not as satisfying.

Help Students Feel Satisfied
With Their Learning Outcomes

An important part of motivating students to learn is to enable students to feel satisfied with their learning outcomes. This can be done by drawing attention to successes they have experienced and by helping students recognize their efforts and improvements through time.

• *Draw attention to the successes that students have achieved.* Displays and announcements about the work of individual students or groups draw attention to the successes that students have experienced. In addition, you can make statements about class progress toward achieving goals and about the students' overall performance.

TEACHERS IN ACTION

Applause to Recognize Successes

*Jane E. Gurnea, third-grade teacher,
Las Cruces, New Mexico*

My third-grade students are required to share orally in large-group, small-group, and individual learning settings. I help establish comfort levels early in the school year by having students pat themselves on the back, shake hands with neighbors, and take bows for hard work, correct answers, or risk-taking efforts. As a result, every student is eager to share orally.

Applause is often spontaneous as the students learn to show appreciation for each other's efforts. When a non-English-speaking student volunteers to share orally and a classmate says, "Take a bow," I am overwhelmed by their recognition of achievement. Recognition from peers is worth as much as, and often more than, recognition generated by the teacher.

• *Help students attribute achievement to effort.* For students to obtain feelings of satisfaction about their academic work, they must actually be successful in various ways. Success doesn't just happen—students must put forth effort. They need to see that their effort is related to their achievements and their feelings of success.

You can help students recognize that achievement is related to effort by drawing attention to the effort they exert in certain tasks. For example, when a student has achieved a better report card grade, you could say, "Gina, coming in for extra help and putting in extra study time really paid off during this grading period. You raised your grade by 14 points. Congratulations!"

Statements drawing attention to effort can also be made during single class sessions. In an art class, you might say, "Reggie, your careful application of the watercolors has helped you show realistic images." The student is reinforced for specific actions and effort and is likely to continue those same actions.

• *Help students recognize that knowledge and skill development are incremental.* Students may not see that each small step they take helps them become more knowledgeable and skilled. If they recognize the importance of each small step, they will realize that their learning is incremental, and they will have more feelings of success and satisfaction.

To help students recognize this, show how their understanding of each part of the subject matter contributes to their understanding of the whole. For example, when teaching students how to do a layup in basketball, help them recognize and practice each important part of the actions—dribbling, dribbling while running, raising the proper foot and arm when releasing the ball, and so on. Students realize that their skill development is incremental, and they can feel satisfaction as they successfully perform each step of the process. Even reading a novel to elementary students one chapter a day shows students that information is incremental.

Use Mistakes and
Redoing Work As Learning Opportunities

Students need to see that their errors are a normal part of learning and that they can improve their thinking and understanding by examining their errors (Ames, 1992; Blumenfeld et al., 1992; Stipek, 1998). You can provide opportunities for students to improve their academic work and to redo assignments as a way to motivate students to learn and to foster learning goals.

- *Treat errors and mistakes as a normal part of learning.* Your response to student errors and mistakes can set the tone for the students. If you treat mistakes as a normal part of learning and see them as a way to improve understanding, then students will likely adopt the same perspective. This takes the pressure off students, and it reinforces the concept that learning is incremental.
- *Use mistakes as a way to help students check their thinking.* Instead of just seeing how many questions they got wrong, students should be given the opportunity to examine their mistakes and to identify the errors in their understanding. This process will help lead to improved student learning.
- *Provide opportunities for improvement or for redoing assignments.* After examining their mistakes, students should have opportunities to correct their mistakes and to improve their performance. In this way, student learning is fostered. You may provide students with the chance to redo assignments or retake quizzes as a means to promote understanding. You might ask students to show something they learned from an error, perhaps through a reflection sheet.

Press Students to Think

Students need feedback to help improve their thinking and understanding of the content. You can press students to think during the lessons through your feedback and expectations for lesson

Table 5.1   Motivational Strategies Concerning Evaluation and Recognition

1. *Establish Evaluation Expectations and Criteria*
   a. Develop an evaluation system that focuses on effort, individual improvement, and mastery, rather than on work completion, getting the right answer, or comparisons with others.
   b. Make rewards contingent on effort, improvement, and good performance.
   c. Avoid norm-referenced grading systems.
   d. Describe evaluations as feedback to show how well students are doing.
   e. Emphasize the factors that students have control over as affecting their performance.
   f. Minimize the use of competition and comparisons with others when evaluating students.
   g. If competition is used, make sure all students have an equal chance of "winning."
   h. Avoid unnecessary differential treatment of high and low achievers.

2. *Select Procedures for Monitoring and Judging*
   a. Use several approaches to evaluation to give students information about their accomplishments.
   b. Provide frequent opportunities for students to respond to and to receive feedback about their academic work.
   c. Provide immediate feedback about student performance whenever possible.
   d. Limit practices that focus students' attention on extrinsic reasons for engaging in tasks (e.g., close monitoring, deadlines, threats of punishment, and competition).
   e. Make evaluation private, not public.

3. *Decide When to Give Feedback and Rewards*
   a. Give some rewards early in the learning experience.
   b. Use motivating feedback following correct responses to maintain the quantity of performance.
   c. Provide corrective feedback when it will be immediately useful to improve the quality of performance.

Table 5.1 (Continued)

4. *Select the Types of Feedback and Rewards*
   a. Use verbal praise and informative feedback.
   b. Offer rewards as incentives but only when necessary.
   c. Make rewards contingent on mastery or a performance level that each student can achieve with effort.
   d. Provide substantive, informative evaluation that is based on mastery, rather than on social norms.

5. *Help Students Feel Satisfied With Their Learning Outcomes*
   a. Draw attention to the successes that students have achieved.
   b. Help students attribute achievement to effort.
   c. Help students recognize that knowledge and skill development are incremental.

6. *Use Mistakes and Redoing Work As Learning Opportunities*
   a. Treat errors and mistakes as a normal part of learning.
   b. Use mistakes as a way to help students check their thinking.
   c. Provide opportunities for improvement and for redoing assignments.

7. *Press Students to Think*
   a. Require students to explain and justify their answers.
   b. Prompt, reframe the question, or break it into smaller parts when students are unsure, and probe students when their understanding is unclear.
   c. Monitor for comprehension, rather than procedural correctness, during activities.
   d. Encourage responses from all students.
   e. Supplement short-answer assignments in commercial workbooks with questions that require higher levels of student thinking.

Academic and Behavioral Expectations

The academic and behavioral expectations that you have for students will translate into a number of decisions concerning classroom management and discipline and the classroom climate you intend to create. All these factors will influence students' motivation to learn. To address these issues, the following specific strategies are discussed in this chapter:

1. Help students expect to be successful
2. Establish appropriate rules and procedures
3. Provide assistance to keep students on task
4. Intervene when students misbehave

Help Students Expect to Be Successful

Help students see that they can be successful through personal control (Keller, 1983). Students' motivation is enhanced when they maintain expectations for success. Techniques used for this purpose address the students' inner need to be competent, and thus the techniques are intrinsically satisfying. The following approaches can help students maintain expectations for success.

• *Have high academic expectations for all students.* Students need to experience success. Successful experiences help develop feelings of self-worth and confidence toward new activities. Students' motivation to learn, however, is greatly influenced by their teachers' expectations for student learning, and teacher expectations can be a self-fulfilling prophecy in the classroom.

If you have high academic expectations for all students, you will communicate that in many ways, and students will often rise to the occasion. If you have lower expectations for some students, however, you may have different interactions with these students (Brophy, 1983b)—fewer personal contacts, more criticism for incorrect answers, less feedback on student work, and other actions. To avoid these problems, simply have high expectations for all students.

• *Indicate the requirements for students to be successful in their instructional tasks.* Students need to know what is expected of them in their academic tasks to be able to complete these tasks. When you provide specific and complete descriptions of task requirements, students will know what is expected of them, and this will increase their expectancy for success in the task (Good & Brophy, 2000; Keller, 1983).

• *Provide abundant opportunities for students to experience success.* If students have had a number of successful academic experiences in your class, then they will more likely enter each new instructional task expecting to be successful once again. Increasing experience with success actually increases student expectancy for success (Keller, 1983).

• *Have students set short-term goals.* Students will work harder for goals they set themselves than for goals set by someone else. Students who set short-term goals have higher intrinsic interest, higher feelings of self-efficacy, and improved performance in the content area (Zimmerman, 1989). Attainment of short-term goals seems to enhance both learning and motivation. When students achieve their goals, they have a sense of mastery that serves to make the activities more interesting (Ames, 1992).

You should help students identify short-term goals and set appropriate standards for judging their own progress. Goal setting

- *Select the rules.* After considering the need for classroom rules, you are ready to select rules that are appropriate for your classroom. Sample rules include (a) follow the teacher's directions; (b) obey all school rules; (c) speak politely to all people; and (d) keep your hands, feet, and objects to yourself.

For departmentalized settings and grade levels, some rules about materials and starting class are often used, such as (a) bring all needed materials to class, and (b) be in your seat and ready to work when the bell rings at the start of the period. Guidelines for identifying classroom rules are displayed in Table 6.1.

TEACHERS IN ACTION

Rules and Consequences

Peggy Shields, high school mathematics teacher,
Pittsburgh, Pennsylvania

I select four rules that are stated positively, identifying what students are expected to do, rather than what they shouldn't do. These rules are (1) do not disrupt the learning of others, (2) be prompt, (3) be ready (physically and mentally), and (4) be seated. I emphatically state that students do not have the right to interfere with anyone else's learning.

Consequences are essential to the rules. They should be hierarchical and, more important, be things that are under control of the teacher. For example, do not include a 1-day suspension as a consequence if you do not have the authority to suspend students. My consequences are (a) a warning, (b) detention after school, (c) a phone call to the student's home, and (d) a referral to the office.

Don't make idle threats. Students know from others if you really call the students' homes. Respect from students is essential in a well-managed classroom. Respect is earned; it is not automatic. Many inexperienced teachers demand respect before they have earned it. Be patient. If you are fair and consistent, respect will follow.

Table 6.1 Guidelines for Selecting Classroom Rules

---

1. Make classroom rules consistent with school rules.

2. Involve students in making the rules to the degree that you are comfortable and to the degree that the students' age level and sophistication permit.

3. Identify appropriate behaviors and translate them into positively stated classroom rules.

4. Focus on important behavior.

5. Keep the number of rules to a minimum (3-6).

6. Keep the wording of each rule simple and short.

7. Have rules address behaviors that can be observed.

8. Identify rewards when students follow the rules and consequences when they break them.

• *Select rewards and consequences.* Both rewards and penalties need to be identified for the classroom rules. Rewards may include a variety of reinforcers such as social reinforcers, activities and privileges, tangible reinforcers, and token reinforcers. Students need to be told that these reinforcers will be delivered if they follow the rules.

Similarly, students need to be told what consequences will be delivered if they choose to break a rule. When a student gets off task, first provide situational assistance in an effort to get the student back to work. If the student stays off task, then you should deliver mild responses such as nonverbal and verbal actions. If that doesn't work, you can move to moderate responses (logical consequences and various types of behavior modification) and then implement severe responses (reprimands and overcorrection) if needed.

• *Teach and review the rules.* After the classroom rules have been identified, rules should be taught in the first class session as if they

---

Table 6.2 Guidelines for Teaching and Reviewing Classroom Rules

---

1. Plan to discuss and teach the rules in the first class session.

2. Discuss the need for the rules.

3. Identify specific expectations relevant to each rule; provide examples and emphasize the positive side of the rules.

4. Inform students of the consequences when rules are followed and also when they are broken.

5. Verify understanding.

6. Send a copy of your discipline policy home to parents and to the principal.

7. Post the rules in a prominent location.

8. Remind the class of the rules at times other than when someone has just broken a rule.

9. Review the rules regularly.

---

were subject matter content. This discussion should include an explanation of the rules, rehearsal, feedback, and reteaching. It is important that the students recognize the rationale for the rules and are provided with specific expectations for each rule. Specific guidelines for teaching and reviewing classroom rules are listed in Table 6.2.

- *Obtain commitments.* After teaching the rules to the students, you should have your students express their understanding of the rules and indicate their intention to follow the rules. Although this can be done in a variety of ways, one of the most effective is to have students sign a copy of the paper that lists the rules and includes a statement such as "I am aware of these rules and understand them." In this way, each student makes an affirmation of the rules. You can keep these signed sheets. Extra copies of the rules could be given to students to place in their desks or notebooks.

Sending the discipline policy home to parents is another means of obtaining a commitment to the policy. In this way, parents are informed of the policy at the start of the school year. Parents can contact you if they have any concerns or questions about the discipline policy. If not, the parents are asked to sign and return a form that states that they are aware of the rules and understand them (similar to the form their child could sign at school).

Procedures

Procedures are approved ways to achieve specific tasks in the classroom. They are intended to help students accomplish a particular task, rather than prevent inappropriate behavior as in the case of rules (Burden, 1995). Procedures may be identified to direct activities such as handing in completed work, sharpening a pencil, using the rest room, and putting away supplies. The use of procedures, or routines, has several advantages (Leinhardt, Weidman, & Hammond, 1987): They increase the shared understanding for an activity between you and students, reduce the complexity of the classroom environment to a predictable structure, and allow for efficient use of time.

Some procedures may be sufficiently complex or critical, such as safety procedures for a laboratory or student notebook requirements, that you should provide students with printed copies of the procedures. Many procedures, however, are not written because they are simple or their specificity and frequency of use allow students to learn them rapidly. Just as with rules, it is important to clearly state the procedures, discuss the rationale for them, and provide opportunities for practice and feedback, where appropriate.

• *Examine the need for procedures.* As a first step, you must examine the need for procedures in your classroom. What activities or actions would benefit from having a procedure that would regularize student conduct in the performance of that action? To answer this key question, think about all the actions that take place in the classroom and identify those that would benefit from having an associated procedure.

Fortunately, you do not need to start from scratch in doing this assessment because research studies of classroom management in K-12 classrooms have resulted in a framework that can be used to examine and identify typical classroom procedures. A number of the specific areas that might need classroom procedures are displayed in Table 6.3, some of which are adapted from Emmer, Evertson, Clements, and Worsham (2000); Evertson, Emmer, Clements, and Worsham (2000); Jones and Jones (1998); Weinstein (1996); and Weinstein and Mignano (1997).

- *Select the procedures.* When examining the items in Table 6.3, you need to consider the unique circumstances in your classroom. The grade level, maturity of the students, your preference for order and regularity, and other factors may be taken into account when deciding which items will need a procedure. It may turn out that you will select many items from the table because these items involve fairly standard actions in many classrooms.

After selecting the items needing a procedure, decide specifically what each procedure will be. You could draw on your own experiences when deciding on the specific procedures. You might recollect your own schooling experiences, your observations of other classrooms, your conversations with other teachers, and your own teaching experience when determining what specific procedures would be appropriate and efficient.

- *Teach and review the procedures.* Students shouldn't have to guess if they need to raise their hands during a discussion and shouldn't have to interpret subtle signals from you to determine what you want them to do. Several steps serve as guides when teaching and reviewing classroom procedures with the students: (a) Explain the procedure immediately prior to the first time the activity will take place, (b) demonstrate the procedure, (c) practice and validate understanding, (d) give feedback, (e) reteach as needed, (f) review the procedures with the students prior to each situation for the first few weeks, and (g) review the procedures after long holidays.

Table 6.3 Areas Needing Classroom Procedures

1. *Room Use Procedures*
   a. Teacher's desk and storage areas
   b. Student desks and storage for belongings
   c. Storage for class materials used by all students
   d. Pencil sharpener, wastebasket, sink, and drinking fountain
   e. Bathroom
   f. Learning stations, computer areas, equipment areas, centers, and display areas

2. *Transitions In and Out of the Classroom*
   a. Beginning the school day
   b. Leaving the room
   c. Returning to the room
   d. Ending the school day

3. *Out-of-Room Procedures*
   a. Bathroom and drinking fountain
   b. Library and resource room
   c. School office
   d. School grounds
   e. Cafeteria
   f. Lockers
   g. Fire or disaster drills

4. *Procedures for Whole-Class Activities and Instruction and/ or Seatwork*
   a. Student participation
   b. Signals for student attention
   c. Talk among students
   d. Making assignments
   e. Distributing books, supplies, and materials
   f. Obtaining help
   g. Handing back assignments
   h. Tasks after work is completed
   i. Makeup work
   j. Out-of-seat procedures

(Continued)

Table 6.3 (Continued)

5. *Procedures During Small-Group Work*
   a. Getting the class ready
   b. Taking materials to groups
   c. Student movement in and out of groups
   d. Expected behavior in groups
   e. Expected behavior out of groups

6. *Beginning the Class Period*
   a. Attendance check
   b. Previously absent students
   c. Late students
   d. Expected student behavior
   e. What to bring to class
   f. Movement of student desks

7. *Ending the Class Period*
   a. Summarizing content
   b. Putting away supplies and materials
   c. Getting ready to leave

8. *Other Procedures*
   a. Classroom helpers
   b. Behavior during delays or interruptions
   c. Split lunch period

Provide Assistance to Keep Students On Task

Students sometimes pause from the instructional task to look out the window, daydream, fiddle with a comb or other object, or simply take a brief mental break from the work. In these examples, the students are not misbehaving—they are simply off task for a short time. You should take steps to draw the student back into the lesson and to keep the student on task.

To communicate to the student that you have noticed the off-task behavior, you should first provide *situational assistance*—actions designed to help the students cope with the instructional situation and to keep them on task or to get them back on task before problems worsen (Burden, 1995). Problem behaviors can be stopped early before they escalate or involve other students.

In an early work on behavior management intervention, Redl and Wineman (1957) identified 12 behavior-influence techniques designed to manage surface behaviors. Their work has been expanded and reorganized by others (e.g., Burden, 1995; Levin & Nolan, 2000; Weinstein, 1996; Weinstein & Mignano, 1997). The organization of this section represents a synthesis of these suggested techniques.

- *Remove distracting objects.* Students sometimes bring to school objects that may be distracting, such as combs, keys, or magazines. When you see that an object is keeping a student from the assigned tasks, simply walk over to the student and collect the object. The student should be quietly informed that the object can be picked up after class. Be kind and firm; no discussion is necessary. Inform students that they should store such objects in an appropriate place before school.
- *Provide support with routines.* Students appreciate and often find comfort in knowing what is going to happen during the class or during the day. They like to know where, when, why, and with whom they will be at various times. It is helpful to announce and post the daily schedule. Changes in the schedule should be announced in advance, if possible. Even for a single lesson, students often appreciate knowing at the start what activities are planned for the lesson. Knowing the schedule provides students with a sense of security and direction. Routines for entering and leaving the classroom, distributing classroom papers and materials, and participating in group work contribute to this sense of security.
- *Reinforce appropriate behaviors.* Students who have followed the directions can be praised. This communicates to the student who is off task what is expected. A statement such as "I'm pleased to see that Juan has his notebook ready for today's lesson" communicates to others what is expected. Appropriate behavior is reinforced while simultaneously giving a signal to students who are off task. Such reinforcement is more commonly used in elementary classrooms, and middle and secondary students may consider this approach to be a little juvenile.

- *Boost student interest.* Student interest may wane in time as the lesson proceeds. You should express interest in the student's work when the student shows signs of losing interest or being bored. Offer to help, noting how much work has been completed, noting how well done the completed part of the task is, or discussing the task. These actions can help bring the student back on task. Interest boosting is often needed when students do individual or small-group classwork.

For example, when a student working in a small group appears to be off task, you could walk over and ask how the group is doing. Also, you might ask the student a question about the group's progress. Take a matter-of-fact, supportive attitude when trying to boost student interest.

- *Provide cues.* Sometimes, all the students are asked to do one thing, such as to prepare their materials or to clean up at the end of class, and cues can be given in these cases. *Cues* are signals that it is time for a selected behavior. For example, you may close the door at the start of class as a cue that instruction is about to begin and that everyone is expected to have all materials ready. The lights could be flipped or a bell sounded to signal time to begin cleanup or to finish small-group work.

For these situations, you can select an appropriate cue and explain its use to the students. Using the same cues consistently usually results in quick responses. You are conveying behavioral expectations and encouraging constructive, on-task behavior.

- *Help students over hurdles.* Students who are experiencing difficulty with a specific task need help in overcoming that problem— helping them over a hurdle—to keep them on task. Hurdle helping may consist of encouraging words from you, an offer to assist with a specific task, or making available additional materials or equipment. For example, in a seatwork activity in which students need to draw several elements, including some straight lines, you might notice that one student is becoming upset that her lines are not straight. You could help her by handing her a ruler. In this way, you help before the student gives up on the assignment or becomes disruptive.

• *Redirect the behavior.* When students show signs of losing interest, you can ask them to answer a question, to do a problem, or to read as a means of drawing them back into the lesson. Students should be treated as if they were paying attention and should be reinforced if they respond appropriately. It is important not to embarrass or ridicule students by saying that they would have been able to answer the question if they had been paying attention. Simply by asking a content-related question, students will recognize that you are trying to draw them back into the lesson. Redirecting student behavior back into the lesson discourages off-task behavior.

• *Alter the lesson.* Lessons sometimes do not go as well as you would like, and students may lose interest in the lesson for a variety of reasons. The lesson needs to be altered in some way when students are seen daydreaming, writing notes to friends, yawning, stretching, or moving around in their seats. This allows for a change of activities such as small-group discussions or games that students like and that require their active participation. Select a different type of activity from the one that has proved to be unsuccessful. When you alter the lesson early, you are able to keep student attention focused on the lesson and maintain order. For example, if a whole-class discussion proves to be unsuccessful, you might have students work in pairs on a related issue that still deals with the lesson's objectives.

In your initial planning, take student interests and abilities into account and provide a variety of activities in each lesson. The need to alter the lesson once under way is thereby minimized. It is helpful to have several types of activities planned in each lesson, some requiring active student participation. Consider the length of time allocated to each activity by taking into account the students' age and maturity.

• *Provide nonpunitive time-out.* Students who become frustrated, agitated, or fatigued may get off task and become disruptive. When you notice this happening, you could provide a nonpunitive time-out. A *time-out* is a period of time in which the student is away from the instructional situation to calm down and reorganize his or her thoughts. The student then returns to the task with a fresh perspective. This time-out is not intended to be a *punitive response*, or a punishment for the off-task behavior.

When a time-out is needed, you could ask the student to run an errand, help you with something, go get a drink, or do some other task not related to the instructional activity. Be alert to students showing signs of frustration and agitation and be ready to respond quickly.

Sometimes, it is useful to have a small area of the room specifically designated for time-outs. This could be a desk placed off in a corner, partly hidden by a filing cabinet. The student could go to this semiprivate area in an effort to calm down and prepare to continue with the lesson. You could suggest that the students be allowed to go to this area when they think they need it. Students who use the corner for nonpunitive time-outs should be allowed to decide themselves when they are ready to return.

• *Modify the classroom environment.* The classroom environment itself may contribute to off-task behavior. The arrangement of the desks, tables, instructional materials, and other items in the classroom may give rise to inefficient traffic patterns or limited views of the instructional areas. Other factors include the boundaries between areas for quiet student and group projects and access to supplies. In addition, both your actions and those of your students may affect their behavior.

Once misbehavior develops, you may need to separate the students or change the setting in some way. Examine the disturbance and identify the element that contributes to it. Modification in the classroom arrangement may include moving tables, student desks, or the storage area.

Intervene When Students Misbehave

Students may misbehave even after you have developed a system of rules and procedures, provided a supportive instructional environment, and given situational assistance to get misbehaving students back on task. In that case, mild responses should be used first to correct the students' behavior. If mild responses are not successful, then use moderate responses.

Mild Responses

Mild responses are nonpunitive ways to deal with misbehavior while providing guidance for appropriate behavior. Nonverbal and verbal mild responses are meant to stop the off-task behavior and to restore order.

Nonverbal Responses

Even with situational assistance, students may get off task. *Nonverbal responses* are taken as a nonpunitive means to get the student back on task. Nonverbal responses may include planned ignoring, the use of nonverbal signals, standing near the student, or touching the student. These approaches are taken in increasing order of teacher involvement and control.

• *Ignore the misbehavior.* Intentionally ignoring minor misbehavior is sometimes the best course of action to weaken the behavior. This is based on the reinforcement principle called *extinction*, that is, if you ignore a behavior and withhold reinforcement, the behavior will lessen and ultimately disappear. Minor misbehaviors that might be ignored are pencil tapping, body movements, hand waving, book dropping, calling out an answer instead of raising a hand, interrupting the teacher, whispering, and so on. Behaviors designed to get your attention or that of their classmates are likely candidates for extinction, or ignoring the behavior.

Ignoring the behavior is best used to control only behaviors that cause little interference to teaching/learning (Brophy, 1988), and it should be combined with praise for appropriate behavior. Extinction is inappropriate for behaviors (e.g., talking out and aggression) reinforced by consequences that you do not control or for behaviors (violence) that cannot be tolerated during the time required for extinction to work (Kerr & Nelson, 1998). If the behavior continues after a reasonable period of planned ignoring, you should be more directive.

There are limitations to ignoring the behavior (Morris, 1985). One risk is that students may conclude that you are not aware of what is happening and may continue the behavior. Although you may ignore the behavior and not give the student the desired attention, other students may give such attention. Furthermore, the student may continue the behavior for a while after you ignore it; if the deliberate ignoring is effective, however, the student will eventually stop the behavior. For some behaviors, extinction is too slow to be of practical value. Aggressive or hostile behaviors may be too dangerous to ignore.

• *Use nonverbal signals.* A nonverbal signal used to communicate to the disrupting student that the behavior is not appropriate is *signal interference.* Signals must be directed at the student. They let the student know that the behavior is inappropriate and that it is time to get back to work.

Nonverbal signal interference may include making eye contact with the student who is writing a note, shaking a hand or finger to indicate not to do some inappropriate action, holding a hand up to stop a student's calling out, or giving the "teacher look." These actions should be done in a businesslike manner. You need to move to the next level of intervention if these disruptive behaviors persist.

TEACHERS IN ACTION

Using Body Language and the "Teacher Look"

Lynne Hagar, high school history and English teacher,
Mesquite, Texas

I am a small woman, but I can effectively control 30 senior students just by using my voice and my body language. When I want a certain behavior to stop, the first thing I do is look at the student. Even if that student is not looking at me, he or she eventually becomes aware that I am staring. Then I point at the student and nonverbally indicate that the behavior is to stop. A finger placed on my lips indicates that talking needs to stop.

Often, a questioning or disapproving look or gesture can stop undesirable behaviors right there. I may have to move into a student's personal space or comfort zone to stop a behavior, but a combination of a look and physical proximity are effective about 90% of the time. I might even casually rest my hand on the student's desk, never stopping teaching, and stay put for a minute or so until I'm sure the student is back on task.

My advice is to practice "the look" in the mirror until you get it right. It shouldn't be a friendly look, but it doesn't have to be angry, either. Learn to say in your manner, "I am in charge here."

Also, move around the classroom. Getting close to your students is essential, not only when you are correcting them but also when you want to reassure them or reinforce their positive feelings about you and your classroom. A friendly touch on the shoulder as you are helping a student with a problem or a hug when a student has a big success can go miles toward cementing your positive relationship with that student.

• *Stand near the student.* Your physical presence near the disruptive student to help the student get back on task is *proximity control.* This is sometimes warranted when you can't get the student's attention to send a signal because the student is so engrossed in an inappropriate action. For example, a student may be reading something other than class-related material or may be writing a note. While doing this, the student may not even look up at you. As a result, signals will not work. While conducting the lesson, walk around the room and approach the student's desk. It is then likely that the student will notice your presence and put the material away without a word being spoken.

Some proximity control techniques may be subtle, such as walking toward the student, whereas other approaches such as standing near the student's desk are more direct. If students do not respond to proximity control, you need to move to a more directive level of intervention.

• *Touch the student.* Without any verbal exchange, you may place a hand on a student's shoulder in an effort to achieve calm, or take a student's hand and escort the student back to his or her seat. These are examples of *touch control*—mild, nonaggressive physical contact that is used to get the student on task. It communicates that you disapprove of the action. Touch control, such as repositioning the student's hand where it belongs on the desk, may redirect the student back into the appropriate behavior.

When deciding whether and how to use touch control, take into account the circumstances of the behavior and the characteristics of the students. Students who are angry or visibly upset sometimes do not want to be touched, and some students do not want to be touched at any time. How well touch will be received depends on where it occurs and how long it lasts. A touch on the back, hand, arm, or shoulder is acceptable to many students, whereas a touch to the face, neck, leg, chest, or other more personal areas is inappropriate. A brief touch is considered acceptable; the longer the touch, the more it becomes inappropriate and may even be considered a threat.

Verbal Responses

Although nonverbal mild responses may be effective, verbal responses can also be used as nonpunitive, mild responses to misbehavior. Their purpose is to get the student back on task with limited disruption and intervention. Various verbal responses are described below.

• *Call on the student during the lesson.* You can recapture a misbehaving student's attention by using his or her name in the lesson, such as "Now, in this next example, suppose that John had three polygons that he . . . ." You could ask a question of the student to recapture the student's attention. Calling on the student in these ways allows you to communicate that you know what is going on and to capture the student's attention without citing the misbehavior.

Be cautious—students' dignity should be preserved. If you call on students in these ways only when they misbehave, they will sense that you are just waiting to catch them misbehaving, and this strategy will backfire by creating resentment (Good & Brophy, 2000).

• *Use humor.* Humor can be used as a gentle reminder to students to correct their behavior. Humor directed at the situation or even at yourself can defuse tension that might be created because of the misbehavior. It can depersonalize the situation and thus help resolve the problem.

You must be careful that the humor is not sarcastic. Sarcasm includes statements that are directed at or make fun of the student; these statements are intended to "put down" or cause pain to the student. Instead, humor should be directed at or make fun of the situation. The student may then reconsider his or her actions and get back on task.

• *Send an I-message.* An I-message verbally prompts appropriate behavior without giving a direct command. Gordon (1991) developed this technique for verbally dealing with misbehavior. An I-message is a statement you make to a misbehaving student.

An I-message has three parts: (a) a brief description of the misbehavior, (b) a description of its effects on you or the other students, and (c) a description of your feelings about the effects. For example, you might say, "When you tap your pen on the desk during the test, it makes a lot of noise, and I am concerned that it might distract other students."

I-messages are intended to help students recognize that their behavior has consequences for other students and that you have genuine feelings about the actions. Because I-messages leave the decision about changing one's behavior up to the students, they are likely to promote a sense of responsibility.

• *Use positive phrasing.* Positive phrasing is used when inappropriate, off-task behavior allows you to highlight positive outcomes for appropriate behavior (Shrigley, 1985). This usually takes the form of "When you do X (behave in a particular appropriate way), then you can do Y (a positive outcome)." For example, when a student is out of her seat, you might say, "Renee, when you return to your seat, then it will be your turn to pick up the supplies."

Through the use of positive phrasing, you redirect students from disruptive to appropriate behavior by simply stating the positive outcomes. In the long run, students begin to believe that proper behavior does lead to positive outcomes.

• *Remind students of the rules.* Each classroom needs to have a set of rules governing student behavior, along with a set of consequences for breaking them. When students see that consequences of misbehavior are in fact delivered, reminders of the rules can help them get back on task because they do not want the consequences. When one student is poking another student, for example, you might say, "Dolores, the classroom rules state that students must keep their hands and feet to themselves."

This reminder often ends the misbehavior because the student does not want the consequence. If the inappropriate behavior continues, you must deliver the consequence; otherwise, the reminder will be of little value because students will recognize that there is no follow-through.

• *Give the students choices.* Some students feel defensive when confronted about their misbehavior. To prevent this, you can give them choices about resolving the problem. This allows the students to feel that they settled the problem without appearing to back down. All the choices that you give to the students should lead to resolution of the problem. If a student is talking to another nearby student, you might say, "Harvey, you can turn back in your seat and get back to your project, or you can take the empty seat at the end of the row." In this way, Harvey has a choice, but the result is that he gets back to work either in his seat or in the seat at the end of the row.

TEACHERS IN ACTION

Giving Students Choices

Terri Jenkins, instruction, Augusta, Georgia

Avoiding conflict is important for classroom survival. This is especially true if the student is trying to seek power or attention. By giving the student a choice in resolving a problem, you defuse the situation and avoid a conflict.

For example, a student may be talking with a neighbor while you are giving instructions. You might say, "Brian, I really need quiet while I am giving directions so that everyone can hear. You have a choice: (1) You may remain where you are and stop talking to Mary, or (2) you may reseat yourself somewhere else in the classroom. Thanks." Then you should walk away.

In this way, students have the power to make a choice. They do not feel challenged and usually respond appropriately. The behavior stops, and little instructional time is lost. Choices should not be punitive or rewarding; they should be designed to stop the misbehavior.

When giving choices, you should be polite and courteous, being careful that the tone of your voice is emotionless. After stating the choices, you should say thank you and then walk away from the student. In this way, it becomes obvious that you expect the student to comply.

• *Ask, "What should you be doing?"* Glasser (1992) proposes that teachers ask disruptive students questions in an effort to direct them back to appropriate behavior. When a student is disruptive, you might ask, "What should you be doing?" This question can have a positive effect because it helps redirect the student back to appropriate behavior.

Of course, some students may not answer this question honestly or not reply at all. In that case, you should make statements related to the question. For example, "Keith, you were swearing and name-calling. That is against our classroom rules. You should not swear or call others names." If the student continues to break the rule, then appropriate consequences should be delivered.

• *Give a verbal reprimand.* A straightforward way to have the students stop misbehaving is to simply ask or direct them to do so. This is sometimes called a *desist order* or a *reprimand* and is given to decrease unwanted behavior. Verbal reprimands are effective with many mild and moderate behavior problems, but by themselves are less successful with severe behavior disorders (Kerr & Nelson, 1998).

A *direct appeal* involves a courteous request for the student to stop the misbehavior and to get back on task. You might say, "Martina, please put away the comb and continue with the class assignment." A direct appeal often gives the student a sense of ownership for deciding to get back on task and to do as you requested. The student feels a sense of responsibility.

As an alternative, you could use a *direct command* in which you take the responsibility and give a direction in a straightforward manner, such as "Wayne, stop talking with your friends and get to work on the lab activity." With the direct appeal and the direct command, the student is expected to comply with your directions. If the student defies your request or command, you must be prepared to deliver an appropriate consequence.

Soft reprimands, audible only to the misbehaving student, are more effective than loud reprimands in reducing disruptive classroom behavior (Kerr & Nelson, 1998). Soft, private reprimands do not call the attention of the entire class to the misbehaving student and also may be less likely to trigger emotional reactions.

Moderate Responses

Following situational assistance and mild nonverbal and verbal responses, students might continue to misbehave. In that case, moderate responses should be used to correct the problem.

Moderate responses are intended to be *punitive ways* to deal with misbehavior *by removing desired stimuli* to decrease the occurrence of the inappropriate behavior. Moderate responses include logical consequences and behavior modification techniques. Because student behaviors that warrant moderate responses are more problematic than mild misbehaviors, it is often useful to discuss specific problems with the principal, other teachers, or the school counselor. Parents can be contacted at any point in an effort to inform them of their child's actions and to solicit their help.

A *logical consequence* is an event that is arranged by the teacher that is directly and logically related to the misbehavior (Dreikurs, Grunwald, & Pepper, 1982). The consequences should be reasonable, respectful, and related to the student action. For instance, if a student leaves paper on the classroom floor, the student must pick the paper up off the floor. If a student breaks the rule of speaking out without raising his or her hand, you would ignore the response and call on a student whose hand is up. If a student marks on the desk, the student is required to clean the marks off. Students are more likely to respond favorably to logical consequences because they do not consider the consequences mean or unfair.

You may tell the student what the consequence is right after the behavior occurs. For example, "Milton, you left the study area a mess. You need to clean it up at the end of class." As an alternative, you may give the student a choice when inappropriate behavior is noticed. This tells the student that the inappropriate behavior must be changed or, if it isn't changed, that a particular consequence will occur. For example, you may say, "Joellen, you have a choice of not bothering students near you or having your seat changed."

When given a choice, students will often stop the inappropriate behavior. This approach can be effective because the student feels a sense of ownership in solving the problem, and the issue is over quickly. Of course, if the problem behavior continues, you must deliver the consequence that you stated to the student.

At the start of the school year, you should think of two or three logical consequences for each of the classroom rules and inform students of these consequences. Logical, reasonable consequences are preplanned, and you are not under the pressure of thinking up something appropriate at the time the misbehavior occurs.

Because of the variety of rules that you might develop, you might select a wide range of logical consequences; some may be considered behavior modification approaches. Examples of applying logical consequences include the following.

- *Withdraw privileges.* As a regular part of the classroom activities, you may provide your students with a number of special privileges, such as a trip to the library, use of a computer, use of special equipment or a game, and service as a classroom helper. If the misbehavior relates to the type of privilege offered, a logical consequence would be to withdraw the privilege. For example, if a student mishandles some special equipment, then the student would lose the privilege of using the equipment.
- *Change the seat assignment.* Students may talk, poke, or interact with other students in nearby seats. Sometimes, a problem occurs because certain students are seated near each other. Other times, just the placement of the seats enables easy interaction. If inappropriate interaction occurs, a logical consequence would be to relocate the student's seat.
- *Have the student write reflections on the problem.* It is often useful to ask the student to reflect on the situation to help the student recognize the logical connection between the behavior and the consequences. You may ask the student to provide written responses to certain questions; this might be done during a time-out.

Questions may include these: What is the problem? What did I do to create the problem? What should happen to me? What should I do next time to avoid a problem? Other questions may require the student to describe the rule that was broken, why the student chose to misbehave, who was bothered by the misbehavior, what more appropriate behavior could be chosen next time, and what should happen to the student the next time the misbehavior occurs.

Written responses to these or similar questions help students see their behavior more objectively and promote more self-control. You may choose to have the student sign and date the written responses for future reference. The written responses can be useful if the parents need to be contacted at a later time.

TEACHERS IN ACTION

Using an OOPS Sheet for Reflections

Lisa Bietau, fourth-grade teacher,
Manhattan, Kansas

When my students misbehave, I sometimes ask them to fill out an OOPS Sheet to have them reflect on their behavior. OOPS stands for "Outstanding Opportunity for a Personal Stretch." The sheet has a space for the student's name and date at the top. The student needs to fill in several other areas: (1) Describe the problem. (2) What other choices did you have to settle the situation without difficulty? (3) How might you handle this differently if it happens again?

After the student fills out the OOPS Sheet, I meet with the student privately to briefly discuss the situation and to review the options and solutions that the student wrote. This reflection and discussion with me help the students understand my expectations and recognize that they have a responsibility to consider reasonable options when they meet a challenging situation.

I sign the OOPS Sheet and make a copy for my files. The original is then sent home with the student to obtain the parent's signature. All the student's privileges are suspended until the signed sheet is returned. If the sheet is not returned the next day, I call the parents and send another copy home, if necessary. I have found that students show more self-control after completing the OOPS Sheet.

- *Place the student in a time-out.* Sometimes, a student is talking or disrupting the class in a way that interferes with the progress of the lesson. In such a case, the student could be excluded from the group; this is called a *time-out.* Removing the student from the group is a logical consequence of interfering with the group. An area of the room should be established as the time-out area, such as a desk in a corner or partly behind a filing cabinet. As a general rule, a time-out should last no longer than 10 minutes.
- *Hold the student for detention.* Detaining or holding back students when they normally would be free to go and do other things deprives students of free time and perhaps the opportunity to socialize with other students. Detention may include remaining after class or staying after school.

Detention can be a logical consequence for student behaviors that waste class time. A student might be asked to work on the social studies paper that wasn't completed during class because of inappropriate behavior. Students will soon see the logic that time wasted in class will have to be made up later on their own time in detention.

Make sure the student understands the reasons for the detention. It should logically fit the offense, and the time should not be excessive—20 to 30 minutes after school is reasonable. Confer with the student and work out a plan to help the student avoid detention in the future and move toward self-control.

Detention after school can be viewed as unreasonable if the student misses the school bus and is subjected to the hazards of the highway on the way home, or if the parents instructed the student to return home immediately after school. Consider these and related issues when preparing to use after-school detention.

- *Contact the parents.* If a student shows a pattern of repeated misbehavior, then you may need to contact the parents or guardians. The logic here is that if all earlier attempts to extinguish the misbehavior do not work, it is appropriate to go to a higher authority. Notify parents by a note or letter informing them of the problem and soliciting their involvement or support. You may choose to call the parents instead. If the situation is fairly serious, a conference with the parents may be warranted.

• *Have the student visit the principal.* In cases of repeated misbehavior or serious misbehavior, such as fighting, students may be sent to the school office to see the principal. The principal may talk with the student in an effort to use his or her legitimate authority to influence the student to behave properly. Some schools have specific procedures to be followed when students are sent to the principal. When the behavior problems reach this point, the parents and additional personnel, including the school counselor or psychologist, need to be consulted to help the student.

Table 6.4 summarizes strategies for helping students expect to be successful, establishing appropriate rules and procedures, providing assistance to keep students on task, and intervening when students misbehave.

Summary of Main Points

• Specific approaches concerning academic and behavioral expectations are outlined in Table 6.4.
• *Rules* refer to general behavioral standards or expectations that are to be followed in the classroom. *Procedures* are approved ways to achieve specific tasks in the classroom.
• *Situational assistance* involves actions intended to help the students cope with the instructional situation and to keep them on task.
• *Mild responses* are nonpunitive ways to deal with misbehavior while providing guidance for appropriate behavior. Mild responses may include nonverbal and verbal responses.
• *Moderate responses* are intended to be punitive ways to deal with misbehavior by removing desired stimuli to decrease the occurrence of the inappropriate behavior.

Table 6.4 Summary Concerning Academic and Behavioral
Expectations

1. *Help Students Expect to Be Successful*
    a. Have high expectations for all students.
    b. Indicate the requirements for students to be successful in their instructional tasks.
    c. Provide abundant opportunities for students to experience success.
    d. Have students set short-term goals.
    e. Help students assess their progress toward their goals.
    f. Provide feedback to help students connect success to personal effort and ability.
    g. Use techniques that offer students personal control over success in their instructional tasks.
    h. Provide students with encouraging information about future outcomes.

2. *Establish Appropriate Rules and Procedures*
    a. Examine the need for rules and procedures.
    b. Select the rules and procedures.
    c. Select rewards and consequences for the rules.
    d. Teach and review the rules and procedures.
    e. Obtain commitments for the rules.

3. *Provide Assistance to Keep Students on Task*
    a. Remove distracting objects.
    b. Provide support with routines.
    c. Reinforce appropriate behaviors.
    d. Boost student interest.
    e. Provide cues.
    f. Help students over hurdles.
    g. Redirect the behavior.
    h. Alter the lesson.
    i. Provide nonpunitive time-out.
    j. Modify the classroom environment.

Table 6.4 (Continued)

4. *Intervene When Students Misbehave*
   a. Nonverbal Mild Responses
      (1) Ignore the behavior.
      (2) Use nonverbal signals.
      (3) Stand near the student.
      (4) Touch the student.
   b. Verbal Mild Responses
      (1) Call on the student during the lesson.
      (2) Use humor.
      (3) Send an I-message.
      (4) Use positive phrasing.
      (5) Remind students of the rules.
      (6) Give the students choices.
      (7) Ask the student, "What should you be doing?"
      (8) Give a verbal reprimand.
   c. Moderate Responses
      (1) Withdraw privileges.
      (2) Change the seat assignment.
      (3) Have the student write reflections on the problem.
      (4) Place the student in a time-out.
      (5) Hold the student for detention.
      (6) Contact the parents.
      (7) Have the student visit the principal.

Discussion/Reflective Questions

- How might you help students in your classroom expect to be successful?
- What three to six rules do you have in your classroom? Do they need to be changed?
- What types of nonverbal and verbal responses to misbehavior work best for you in your classroom?

Suggested Activities

- Examine the areas in your classroom that need procedures and decide whether any of your current procedures need to be changed.
- In what ways do you provide situational assistance to keep students on task? How could you improve in this area to monitor and respond more effectively?
- When moderate responses are warranted in your classroom, what responses do you use? Which responses are the most effective? Why? What changes do you need to make?

Motivating
Hard-to-Reach Students

Some students are hard to reach and may require additional attention beyond the preventive motivational strategies already discussed in earlier chapters. Hard-to-reach students may be low achievers who have difficulty keeping up with the schoolwork; students with failure syndrome problems; students who want to protect their self-worth; students who are committed underachievers; or students who are apathetic, uninterested, or even alienated (Brophy, 1997). These students may have expectations about themselves, schoolwork, and learning that were developed through prior experiences with failure.

Some hard-to-reach students may even qualify for special education assistance. Others may be hard to reach because English is not their first language. In all these cases, the usual motivational strategies discussed earlier may not be sufficient to help these students. Specific one-on-one assistance may be needed to address the reasons the students are having difficulty in the first place; then support can be provided to motivate them to learn. For example, second-language teaching involves strategies for language acquisition as well as strategies to motive students to learn the language and the instructional content (Nunan, 1999).

When dealing with hard-to-reach students, use the resource people around you—the principal or assistant principal, psychologists, counselors, special education teachers, team leaders, resource teachers, and teachers who are good at teaching and classroom management. For students who qualify for special education support, take full advantage of the resource people and services provided.

Seeking out assistance from these resource people does not mean that you are incapable or that you have failed. Instead, these resource people often have the unique knowledge and skills to best help hard-to-reach students. Don't let your pride get in the way of securing extra ways to help these students.

The ideas presented in this chapter are based on the assumption that all students are motivated to learn under the right conditions and that you can provide those conditions in your classroom. The following specific approaches are discussed in this chapter:

1. Select a level of difficulty for academic work
2. Structure the instructional tasks, assignments, and work expectations
3. Provide clear, simple directions
4. Follow student interests and learning styles
5. Provide task assistance
6. Teach the students study skills and ways to reach their goals
7. Show caring and give attention and encouragement
8. Provide remedial socialization for discouraged and struggling students
9. Provide tutoring from peers, parents, or others
10. Develop an overall strategy to deal with hard-to-reach students

Select a Level of Difficulty for Academic Work

Hard-to-reach students are more likely to have difficulty with the academic work than are the other students in class. As a result, you need to give special attention to selecting a level of difficulty for the academic work for these students so that they can experience success.

- *Focus on the most basic and necessary learnings.* For each unit, you may supplement the basic, essential content with extra information and activities. Low achievers and other hard-to-reach students, however, may have difficulty covering all that material. It is important to focus their attention and efforts on the most basic and necessary learnings so that they have the fundamentals before moving on to other material. Then, if there is still time, these students can proceed to the supplemental content.

- *Reduce the difficulty of tasks that you assign to struggling students to make success likely.* To maintain their interest, all students—including struggling students and low achievers—need to experience success in the learning activity. Select tasks that the students will be able to handle with a reasonable rate of success within their ability range. This may mean that you need to reduce the level of difficulty in the tasks.

TEACHERS IN ACTION

Modifying the Tasks

Jane E. Gurnea, third-grade teacher,
Las Cruces, New Mexico

Modifying instruction to meet individual needs can be an arduous task. At times, I find myself questioning whether the outcomes are worth the effort. This was answered, however, by one of my third-grade students. Arnulfo began the year as a limited-English speaker. For his learning to be successful, I had to modify his spelling lists to consist of five first-grade words.

After mastering these lists, Arnulfo "graduated" to 10 second-grade words. At the end of the year, he wrote an essay, "I was best at spelling in third grade because I worked hard every week to get an A+ on my tests. And I did!" Are modifications worth the teacher's efforts? Arnulfo and I certainly agree that they are.

when it needs to be done. Time limits could be set for activities that need to be completed in one class period, and a target date for completion could be set for longer-term assignments. You might consider setting a longer time limit than what you really expect the students to need; in that way, students can feel good about themselves when they complete the assignments before the time limit.

- *Make sure that the first part of the assignment is easy and familiar enough to provide initial successful experiences.* When students experience success, they are willing to continue their efforts. For that reason, it is important to enable students to experience success at the start of an assignment to encourage their continued efforts throughout the assignment. Therefore, place content and activities that are easy and familiar to the student at the beginning of a task. Then they will be more willing and prepared to address more challenging content and activities later in the task.

- *Limit distractions.* Students who are having academic difficulties or who have a tendency to get off task may be easily distracted by other actions in the classroom. Even minor actions such as someone walking up to a pencil sharpener might take a student's attention away from the tasks at hand. As a result, try to limit the distractions as much as possible for hard-to-reach students. To do so, you might create some quiet areas in your classroom that have a limited view to the rest of the classroom. Consider other ways in which sound, light, and movement might create distractions.

Provide Clear, Simple Directions

Directions at the beginning of the activity provide hard-to-reach students with information about the specific procedures and completed products expected of them in the activity. Although important for all students, clear, simple directions are even more important for hard-to-reach students.

- *Have a limited number of student actions in the directions.* Rather than providing lengthy directions about many actions that students need to take to complete the assignment, it is better to break the assignment up into shorter parts. Having no more than three student actions for an activity is a good guide. Students may have trouble remembering the guidelines if there are more than three actions in the activity.

• *Describe the directions in the order that students will be required to complete the tasks.* If students are expected to complete certain tasks in order, then you should go through those in the same sequence when giving the directions. In this way, students will be more able to visualize what is expected and complete the directions.

• *Demonstrate the expected actions for students and discuss the needed steps and the thinking involved.* When giving directions, it is often helpful to demonstrate or model the actions that you expect the students to take when they complete the assignment. For example, you might go through a few of the math problems first to show what is to be done before having the students work on a related math assignment.

• *State the type and quality of product expected at the end of the assignment.* Your directions should include a description of the finished product for the assignment, whether it be a worksheet, a drawing, a list of spelling words, or some type of product. You may have some sample completed products to show students to help them fully understand the expectations.

• *Check to see if students understand the directions.* To be sure that students understand the directions, you could have students repeat directions to you to make sure that they know what is supposed to be done. Or you could ask, "Do you have any questions about what you need to do?" Also, be available to answer questions once the students begin the assignments.

Follow Student Interests and Learning Styles

To promote active student involvement in the lesson, special attention needs to be given to the interests and learning styles of hard-to-reach students.

• *Build assignments around student interests.* Students are more interested in the lesson content and in completing expected tasks when the content is linked in some way to their interests and when they see the relevance of the content. A lesson on creative writing, for example, might have students prepare a plot or script for a popular television show they watch.

• *Tailor your instruction to take advantage of the student's strongest learning modality.* Information about learning styles, multiple intelligences, and brain functioning can help you adapt instruction to the students' strongest learning preferences and interests. If a hard-to-reach student works best when discussing an issue with another student, for example, provide opportunities for this to occur.

• *Use various forms of instructional materials to reduce the need to learn only by printed materials.* Low-achieving students and underachievers often are not up to grade level in their reading ability. As was mentioned previously, you should select reading materials at the students' levels. In addition, use additional instructional materials that do not require extensive reading. Videotapes, audiocassettes, computer software, and other nonprint instructional materials enable students to learn without having to read everything.

• *Let students do extra credit work in areas of interest.* Students can be energized if they have an opportunity to explore an area of interest—whether it be about a current movie, a sports figure, or some personal interest. By relating that interest to the academic content in some way and providing the opportunity for extra credit points, students will likely pursue that interest with zeal.

• *Discuss the students' occupational plans and help them see that academic skills are required in those occupations.* Especially for students who are committed underachievers, one useful technique to capture their interest is to discuss their occupational plans as a means to relate the academic content to their occupational interests. When students see the relevance of the content and skills for their occupational interests, their interest can be enhanced.

Provide Task Assistance

Low-achieving or struggling students sometimes need some assistance after attempting to work on a task themselves. Identify the best ways to provide this assistance and to support their learning.

• *Ask students how you might be helpful to them, and then follow through on ways that are feasible.* The best way to find out how you can help students is to ask them. They may offer a number of suggestions, ranging from study guides to videotapes to group projects. From their suggestions, you could select the ways that are the most feasible. This strategy often is effective with committed underachievers because they see that you are working closely with them and that you are on their side (McIntyre, 1989).

• *Help students to identify when they do or do not need help and to seek help when they need it.* Struggling students sometimes do not easily distinguish when they should continue working on the task and when they should seek help. Give students a set of procedures to follow when they encounter difficulties, starting with strategies for diagnosing possible causes of their problem and perhaps solving it on their own. If they cannot solve it on their own, then they should seek help. You may need to encourage them to do so because most students are not willing to seek help overtly (Good, Slavings, Harel, & Emerson, 1987; Newman & Goldin, 1990).

• *Select a signal for when students need help.* When students need your help, they need to attract your attention before you can go to the students to provide the assistance. Give students one or more options to use to signal their need for help unobtrusively. Then get to them as quickly as possible and provide the help that they need (Brophy, 1997).

• *Provide brief help.* When students need assistance, provide brief explanations, questions, or hints that will stimulate the students' thinking about the problem and encourage them to work out the rest of it on their own, rather than simply giving them the answers. This helps the students reach the next level in thinking and problem solving and enables them to learn the knowledge or skill that the task was intended to teach (Butler & Neuman, 1995; Nelson-LeGall, 1987).

• *Monitor students closely and frequently.* Struggling students may have difficulty understanding what to do in an assignment, may make errors in the assignment, or may get off task easily. Because of these factors, it is important to monitor hard-to-reach students closely and frequently to provide the assistance that they need and to keep them on task. To do so, you might build checkpoints into the assignments, such as turning in first drafts that you review to provide feedback.

• *Reteach low achievers using varied and enriched forms of instruction.* Low achievers may not understand the content the first time it is taught, and some reteaching may be necessary to help the students learn the material. The manner in which the content is retaught should be different from the approach used in the initial instruction. If some lecture and a writing assignment were used for initial instruction, for example, then the reteaching might involve videotapes, peer tutoring, or a project. Various instructional approaches in reteaching help reach the students' preferred learning style.

• *Provide students with study guides and related learning supports.* Struggling students often need additional help in learning the material. Although you may choose not to give the whole class a study guide for a unit you are covering, struggling students may benefit greatly from having a study guide or other types of assistance available.

• *Rephrase questions or provide hints when students are unable to respond.* Underachievers and struggling students may have difficulty in making the cognitive connections in the content. Therefore, you may need to provide some hints or clues to help guide students when they are unable to respond to questions. Sometimes, you may need only to rephrase the question, but other times you might need to provide some additional content as a link to the correct answer.

Teach the Students Study Skills and Ways to Reach Their Goals

Study skills are competencies associated with acquiring, recording, organizing, synthesizing, remembering, and using information (Devine, 1987). Students who are hard to reach may not have developed adequate study skills, contributing to their academic problems.

• *Teach study and work skills.* A number of sources present strategies for teaching students how to study (e.g., Bragstad & Stumpf, 1987; Devine, 1987; Gall, Gall, Jacobsen, & Bullock, 1990; Rafoth,

Leal, & DeFabo, 1993). Although all students in your class may benefit from some instruction on study skills, special attention should be given to hard-to-reach students.

• *Have students study or at least talk about study habits with a friend who models motivation to learn and conscientiously works on assignments.* In addition to any instruction you might provide in study skills, you could have hard-to-reach students talk with other students who seem to have good study habits. Or you might have them work together for a while to enable the student to develop additional study skills. Of course, not all students want to be teamed up in this way. As an alternative, cooperative learning groups might provide a similar training opportunity.

• *Teach students to set and strive for reasonable short-term goals and to approach long-term goals through a series of steps.* When students have become accustomed to failure, they may also have low self-concepts about their ability. To address these issues, you can help the students set short-term, realistic goals that are achievable. When the students reach those goals, they will start to recognize that they do indeed have the ability to be successful when they apply reasonable effort (Schunk, 1985).

• *Provide feedback that points out correct procedures, remedies errors, and reassures students that they are developing mastery.* Nothing can be more frustrating for low-achieving students than to find out that they were using the wrong approach as they were working on a number of problems. After hearing that, the students may not even try going through the problems again with the correct procedure. Therefore, it is important to closely monitor low-achieving and struggling students to correct any procedures, remedy any errors, and provide any needed corrective feedback to help students master the material.

Show Caring and
Give Attention and Encouragement

When students see that you have a genuine interest in their well-being, they are more likely to work with you to improve. Showing caring and giving attention and encouragement help the students see your sincere interest in their welfare.

- *Develop close relationships with the students.* Developing close relationships with students who have been causing you a lot of discomfort in the classroom may be a difficult thing to do. Yet the students need to see that someone cares for them and is concerned about their welfare. Show the students that you care about them personally and that you are trying to get through to them because it is in their long-term interest (Brophy, 1997). When they know that you are on their side, they will be more willing to comply with other actions you take to help them.

TEACHERS IN ACTION

Developing a Close Relationship

Janet Roesner, elementary school teacher, Baltimore, Maryland

The key to success in improving achievement and motivating students to learn is building a close working relationship with the students. A positive relationship develops mutual understanding between the teacher and the students. In building this relationship, the teacher begins to understand the students' culture, actions and reactions, and ways of thinking. In turn, the students are able to clearly understand the teacher's expectations in relation to their well-being.

Becky Taylor, fourth-grade teacher, Oregon City, Oregon

Victor was a limited-English student who was often on the verge of exploding or withdrawing and sulking. After trying several approaches with him, the real breakthrough for me came by inviting Victor and two friends to go with my family on a Saturday to the Oregon Museum of Science and Industry. A sparkle in his eye showed me that I had finally succeeded in establishing an effective connection. This resulted in an incredible day of bonding with no unrealistic expectations and no conflicts. It was a day filled with fun and exploration.

Now, when I sense a difficult day for Victor, all it takes is a look into his eyes to reconnect. So make the extra effort, use community resources, but most important, establish deep, meaningful relationships.

• *Call attention to student successes.* When the students are successful, it is important that they receive some positive feedback to reinforce their efforts and to encourage them to continue their work. Provide encouragement and supportive comments in person and on papers, and send positive notes home.

• *Reinforce and build on current accomplishments, rather than emphasize past faults and failures.* Struggling or low-achieving students have likely had a history of academic problems. Instead of referring to those past problems, it is important to draw the students' attention to their current accomplishments and to encourage them to continue their efforts. This strategy is especially useful for committed underachievers (Thompson & Rudolph, 1992).

• *Encourage students to focus on surpassing their previous day's or week's performance, rather than on competing with classmates.* To help students recognize the progress that they are making, have them compare their performance with their performance level the previous day or the previous week. This enables the students to see their progress and to recognize that progress is incremental.

• *Avoid lecturing, nagging, or threatening.* Students who have a history of academic or behavioral problems probably have heard plenty of lectures about the need to clear up their problems. It is unlikely that nagging, threatening, and lecturing are effective in helping the students develop the commitment to improve. Instead, caring, encouraging approaches will help students see that you are on their side and that you want to work with them because it is in their best interest.

Also, try to say something to the students only once. If students keep hearing the same message over and over, they might consider it nagging. You could videotape yourself to assess your actions. If you need to say something three times, you probably should have less talk and more action to get the students to respond in the desired ways.

• *Avoid subtle expressions that convey an impression of a student's low ability.* Teachers may inadvertently use expressions about a student's low ability, such as overly sympathetic responses for failure, praise for success on easy tasks, and unnecessary help. These messages can be troubling to the student, and they send a negative message about achievement.

Provide Remedial Socialization for Discouraged and Struggling Students

Students who have a history of academic or behavioral problems often need special attention to help them develop the needed attitudes and skills to improve in their academic work.

• *Help students develop and sustain more positive attitudes toward schoolwork.* Students who are struggling with schoolwork, or students who are discouraged or even uninterested, need to develop more positive attitudes toward schoolwork so that they have a commitment to their own improvement. This can be done through conversations with the students about the relevance of the schoolwork to their future occupational interests or their interests outside of school.

TEACHERS IN ACTION

Helping a Discouraged Student

Jackie Huber, high school mathematics teacher,
Phoenix, Arizona

Students respond to praise, compliments, and encouragement. I must know the subject matter but also must have a lot of patience, mental energy, and selflessness. I have found that you have to be encouraging even to the most negative students, or they can make your life miserable. Although you might know the subject matter, you will not be a successful teacher if you can't motivate your students by talking *with* them, not *at* them.

I vividly remember one student. Mike was 15 years old and was on probation for a crime he had committed. He wore the same dirty clothes every day and smelled really bad. His arms were full of self-inflicted cigarette burns, and he had a real "tough guy" chip on his shoulder. Mike never brought a book, paper, or pencil to class; he just folded his arms and slouched in his seat. I decided that I must help him, so I gave

Mike the needed materials and guided him through some of the problems that I had just assigned to the rest of the class.

As he started writing, I could tell that he had not been listening and that he had a great basic instinct for math—and I told him so. I said that if he really wanted to, he could be doing A or B work in no time if we worked together. He went home and told his dad what I had said. The next day, Mike brought his own materials, and I made sure that I noticed and praised him again. He started taking notes and even raised his hand a couple of times asking for help. I again told him that I was proud of him.

Within about 3 weeks, Mike started to bathe, comb his hair, and wear clean clothes to class. The burns on his arms were healing, and he was doing his work regularly. Mike did receive a B on his report card. He was so proud of himself, and he learned that hard work is very rewarding. Working with Mike was a real challenge, but I thought that it was important to help him feel good about himself through praise, compliments, and real encouragement.

• *Help students accept responsibility for their performance and commit themselves to realistic goals.* Underachieving, discouraged, or uninterested students may benefit from counseling sessions designed to let them voice their concerns. These sessions, however, should also include some pressure to help the students accept responsibility for their performance and commit themselves to realistic goals (Blanco & Bogacki, 1988).

• *Help students concentrate on the task at hand, rather than worrying about failure.* Some students with a history of academic problems may continually focus on their failures. It is important to help these students concentrate on the immediate task, rather than reflecting on their past problems (Craske, 1988; Dweck & Elliott, 1983). In this way, students can see their short-term progress, and you have an opportunity to reinforce and encourage the students.

• *Help students cope with failures by retracing their steps to find their mistake or by analyzing the problem to find another approach.* Students who have a history of academic problems may give up when they once again do not perform well, or they may not even try to do much of the work if it is challenging and they can't figure out how to do it (Craske, 1988; Dweck & Elliott, 1983). Help these students cope with these situations by having them retrace their steps to see where they made the mistake. Or you could help the students analyze the problem and seek different ways to solve the problem. These skills should help the students develop more confidence and skills as they approach the academic work.

• *Help students attribute their failures to insufficient effort, lack of information, or use of ineffective strategies, rather than to lack of ability.* Some students give up when they confront academic work that is challenging because they think that they do not have the ability. To help students overcome this conclusion, help them attribute their failures to insufficient effort, a lack of information, or the use of ineffective strategies (Craske, 1988; Dweck & Elliott, 1983). Then help the students increase their effort, gather needed information, and select effective strategies.

TEACHERS IN ACTION

Giving Attention to a Problem Student

*Lynne Hagar, high school history and English teacher,
Mesquite, Texas*

John walked into my classroom at the start of the school year ready to fight me all the way. This pugnacious redhead walked, talked, and acted tough as nails, but when I spoke to him sharply, he blushed. John "knew" that he was going to fail from the beginning. He spoke terrible redneck grammar and pushed and shoved his way through the first few weeks.

How should I handle this firecracker of a student? Experience had taught me that a lot of love and consistency would solve many of his problems. I tried to react calmly to John's insulting comments, trusting that once he began to respond to my teaching, he would show more respect. When he became disruptive, I asked him privately to tell me if I had done something to offend him or to lose his respect. I apologized in advance for having done so. John was surprised that a teacher would be concerned about the reasons for his behavior and astonished that I had admitted that I was capable of doing something wrong.

Once we had a basis for our relationship, I found something to say to John every day—not necessarily a compliment, just an acknowledgment that I recognized he was there. I tried my best to listen—really listen—when John talked to me, making eye contact and coming close to his desk. Sometimes, I touched his arm in a friendly way when he entered the room or laid my hand on his shoulder as I passed his seat. I put long comments on his papers and added stickers when his work began to show improvement.

I soon realized that John attended school every day without fail; it was the best place in his life—the only place where he felt safe enough to express his feelings. I gave John opportunities to let his anger out on paper and to write about his feelings. I found out about things he was proud of and then built writing lessons around subjects such as rodeo riding and fast cars. Talking to the shop teacher gave me insight into the difficult time John had at home. An abusive father and economic hardships that forced him to work long hours at night contributed to John's angry manner. Being rejected by people he loved and trusted had caused him to anticipate failure in his personal relationships as well as in his academic work. I wanted him to learn from me that he was both lovable and capable.

I wish I could say that John became a model student, but he became only an average one, trying hard to please me in all that he did. He still lost his temper at times, blushed when teased, and often spoke without asking. But, John began to reveal the intelligent side of his nature, dropped his aggressive pose, and expressed his affection for me and even, once in a great while, his gratitude for my teaching efforts. I began to love John very much and to care deeply about his success. There's something about struggling with a difficult student and succeeding in gaining the student's trust that gives a teacher a special warmth for that student. It's very rewarding in a unique way.

Provide Tutoring
From Peers, Parents, or Others

Some students may benefit from tutoring to help them understand their academic work. Consider various types of tutoring, and closely monitor the interaction and progress.

* *Provide individual tutoring, as needed, from other students or adults.* When selecting a tutor for a student, consider what type of assistance is needed and what type of person would best serve as a tutor. The student may work best with a peer in the same class or with a student in a different grade or class (Blanco & Bogacki, 1988). At other times, a student may need an adult tutor, who could be a parent volunteer.

* *Keep in close communication with anyone who tutors the student.* After selecting the student's tutor, provide specific guidelines and expectations of the tutor so that the student's needs are met. The tutor may need some orientation or training. Once the tutoring begins, stay in close contact to keep abreast of progress and any problems that might occur.

* *Arrange for collaborative learning with peers so that each student has a unique function to perform.* Cooperative learning groups may help hard-to-reach students, especially committed underachievers, by creating peer pressure to do their part (McIntyre, 1989). By their very nature, cooperative learning groups provide support for each group member, so the hard-to-reach students receive some type of individual assistance.

* *Sit students near classmates who can provide some academic assistance.* Sit low-achieving and hard-to-reach students among average (not superior) classmates with whom they enjoy friendly relationships, and ask these classmates to provide some task assistance and reminders of assignments and due dates. In this way, there are students close by to provide some guidance about the academic work without the low-achieving students having to ask the teacher for assistance with every issue.

Develop an Overall Strategy to
Deal With Hard-to-Reach Students

As was mentioned at the start of this chapter, there are many types of hard-to-reach students, and each type may require a different approach.

- *Establish a plan to deal with each hard-to-reach student.* Because there are different types of hard-to-reach students, you may need to use a different approach with each type. In addition, each student has his or her own personality, academic history, and circumstances to be considered. For these reasons, it is helpful to establish a plan to deal with the unique characteristics of each hard-to-reach student.
- *Work with the student's parents and other resource people in the school.* Establish a rapport with the parents as early as possible, before a problem might occur. When developing a plan for a hard-to-reach student, the student's parents should be contacted so that they can share pertinent information about the student and participate in developing a plan for the student. If behavior modification strategies are used with the student, it is helpful to have the parents' cooperation and assistance. School counselors, psychologists, special education teachers, or other resource people in the school can also be consulted for input and support.
- *Prepare contracts for individual students when necessary.* Formalizing your plan in a written contract with the student often sends the student a message about the seriousness of the situation. Contracts often include statements about the desired behaviors, deadlines for the completion of certain tasks, and reinforcers and punishments, depending on whether the desired actions are or are not met. It is often helpful to collaborate with the student to set goals to be included in the contract. Parents may be involved by withholding or providing performance-contingent rewards.
- *Consider encouraging and instructional strategies for younger underachievers but confrontive and persuasive strategies for older students.* Until students reach age 10 or so, they do not appear to settle into

a pattern of systematic avoidance of responsibility. This suggests that encouraging and instructional strategies may work best for younger underachievers. Confrontive and persuasive strategies, however, may be more effective with older students (Brophy, 1997).

Table 7.1 reviews the ideas discussed in this chapter for carrying out strategies to motivate hard-to-reach students.

Summary of Main Points

- Hard-to-reach students may be low achievers who have difficulty keeping up with the schoolwork; students with failure syndrome problems; students who want to protect their self-worth; students who are committed underachievers; or students who are apathetic, uninterested, or even alienated.
- Specific approaches to motivate hard-to-reach students are outlined in Table 7.1.

Discussion/Reflective Questions

- What are the characteristics of hard-to-reach students with whom you have worked?
- What techniques have you successfully used to motivate hard-to-reach students?
- In what ways would an overall strategy to deal with hard-to-reach students be helpful?

Suggested Activities

- Identify a hard-to-reach student you worked with in the past and decide which strategies you might try now to be more successful.
- Talk with other teachers to see how they have successfully worked with hard-to-reach students.
- As you develop an overall strategy to deal with hard-to-reach students, in what ways might you change your approach to curriculum and instruction and to teaching?

Table 7.1   Motivational Strategies Concerning Hard-to-Reach
Students

1. *Select a Level of Difficulty for Academic Work*
   a. Focus on the most basic and necessary learnings.
   b. Reduce the difficulty of tasks that you assign to struggling students to make success likely.
   c. Increase work expectations gradually.
   d. Allow students to contract for a particular level of performance.
   e. Collect books and instructional materials that address content but are written at easier reading levels for struggling students.
   f. Give marks and report card grades on the basis of effort and production, rather than in relation to the rest of the class.

2. *Structure the Instructional Tasks, Assignments, and Work Expectations*
   a. Make sure that assignments are well structured and that expectations are clearly stated.
   b. Keep assignments short.
   c. Set time limits within which the work should be done.
   d. Make sure that the first part of the assignment is easy and familiar enough to provide initial successful experiences.
   e. Limit distractions.

3. *Provide Clear, Simple Directions*
   a. Have a limited number of student actions in the directions.
   b. Describe the directions in the order that students will be required to complete the tasks.
   c. Demonstrate the expected actions for students and discuss the needed steps and the thinking involved.
   d. State the type and quality of product expected at the end of the assignment.
   e. Check to see if students understand the directions.

4. *Follow Student Interests and Learning Styles*
   a. Build assignments around student interests.

(Continued)

Recommended Readings

Brophy, J. E. (1997). *Motivating students to learn.* New York: McGraw-Hill.

Addresses all aspects of motivation in 10 readable chapters. Well referenced, conceptually sound. Many recommended strategies for applying motivational principles.

Burden, P. R. (1995). *Classroom management and discipline: Methods to facilitate cooperation and instruction.* New York: Longman.

Examines ways to establish and maintain order in the classroom, motivate students and establish a positive learning environment, and respond to misbehavior.

Good, T. L., & Brophy, J. E. (2000). *Looking in classrooms* (8th ed.). New York: Longman.

Includes discussion of many aspects of teaching, including a separate chapter on motivation. Thorough research-based coverage.

McCombs, B. L., & Pope, J. E. (1994). *Motivating hard to reach students.* Washington, DC: American Psychological Association.

Provides a practical set of guidelines to facilitate the learning process as a means to help students be self-motivated.

Meece, J., & McColskey, W. (1997). *Improving student motivation: A guide for teachers and school improvement teams.* Tallahassee, FL:

SouthEastern Regional Vision for Education (SERVE). (345 South Magnolia Dr., Suite D-23, Tallahassee, FL 32301; 800-352-6001)

Provides an overview for engaging students in learning, types of motivation and motivational approaches, strategies for school improvement, and assessing student motivation.

Stipek, D. J. (1998). *Motivation to learn: From theory to practice* (3rd ed.). Boston: Allyn & Bacon.

Includes 12 chapters designed to demonstrate how achievement, motivation theory, and research can help teachers develop autonomous, self-confident learners who enjoy learning activities. Well referenced, thorough, and has an academic tone.

References

Ames, C. (1990). Motivation: What teachers need to know. *Teachers College Record, 91,* 409-421.

Ames, C. (1992). Classrooms: Goals, structures, and student motivation. *Journal of Educational Psychology, 84,* 261-271.

Ames, C., & Ames, R. (1984). Systems of student and teacher motivation: Toward a qualitative definition. *Journal of Educational Psychology, 76,* 535-556.

Aronson, E., & Patnoe, S. (1997). *The jigsaw classroom: Building cooperation in the classroom.* New York: Longman.

Biehler, R. F., & Snowman, J. (1997). *Psychology applied to teaching* (8th ed.). Boston: Houghton Mifflin.

Blanco, R., & Bogacki, D. (1988). *Prescriptions for children with learning and adjustment problems: A consultant's desk reference* (3rd ed.). Springfield, IL: Charles C Thomas.

Blumenfeld, P. C., Puro, P., & Mergendoller, J. R. (1992). Translating motivation into thoughtfulness. In H. Marshall (Ed.), *Redefining student learning: Roots of educational change* (pp. 207-239). Norwood, NJ: Ablex.

Bragstad, B. J., & Stumpf, S. M. (1987). *A guidebook for teaching study skills and motivation* (2nd ed.). Boston: Allyn & Bacon.

Brophy, J. E. (1983a). Conceptualizing student motivation. *Educational Psychologist, 18,* 200-215.

Brophy, J. E. (1983b). Research on the self-fulfilling prophecy and teacher expectations. *Journal of Educational Psychology, 75,* 631-661.

Brophy, J. E. (1987). Synthesis of research on strategies for motivating students to learn. *Educational Leadership, 44,* 40-48.

Brophy, J. E. (1988). Educating teachers about managing classrooms and students. *Teaching and Teacher Education, 4*(1), 1-18.

Brophy, J. E. (1997). *Motivating students to learn.* New York: McGraw-Hill.

Brophy, J. E., & Kher, N. (1986). Teacher socialization as a mechanism for developing student motivation to learn. In R. Feldman (Ed.), *Social psychology applied to education* (pp. 257-288). New York: Cambridge University Press.

Burden, P. R. (1995). *Classroom management and discipline: Methods to facilitate cooperation and instruction.* New York: Longman.

Butler, R. (1987). Task-involving and ego-involving properties of evaluation: Effects of different feedback conditions on motivational perceptions, interest, and performance. *Journal of Educational Psychology, 79,* 474-482.

Butler, R., & Neuman, O. (1995). Effects of task and ego achievement goals on help-seeking behaviors and attitudes. *Journal of Educational Psychology, 87,* 261-271.

Campbell, L., Campbell, B., & Dickinson, D. (1999). *Teaching and learning through multiple intelligences* (2nd ed.). Boston: Allyn & Bacon.

Chapman, C. (1993). *If the shoe fits: How to develop multiple intelligences in the classroom.* Arlington Heights, IL: IRI/Skylight Training & Publishing.

Corno, L., & Rohrkemper, M. M. (1985). The intrinsic motivation to learn in the classroom. In C. Ames & R. Ames (Eds.), *Research on motivation in education* (Vol. 2, pp. 53-90). San Diego, CA: Academic Press.

Covington, M. V., & Omelich, C. L. (1984). Task-oriented versus competitive learning structures: Motivational and performance consequences. *Journal of Educational Psychology, 76,* 1038-1050.

Craske, M. (1988). Improving persistence through observational learning and attributional retraining. *British Journal of Educational Psychology, 55,* 138-147.

Deci, E., & Ryan, R. (1985). *Intrinsic motivation and self-determination in human behavior.* New York: Plenum.

Devine, T. G. (1987). *Teaching study skills: A guidebook for teachers* (2nd ed.). Boston: Allyn & Bacon.

Doyle, W. (1983). Academic work. *Review of Education Research, 53,* 159-200.

Doyle, W. (1986). Classroom organization and management. In M. C. Wittrock (Ed.), *Handbook of research on teaching* (3rd ed., pp. 392-431). New York: Macmillan.

Dreikurs, R., Grunwald, B. B., & Pepper, F. C. (1982). *Maintaining sanity in the classroom: Classroom management techniques* (2nd ed.). New York: Harper & Row.

Dweck, C. S., & Elliott, E. S. (1983). Achievement motivation. In P. Mussen (Ed.), *Handbook of child psychology: Vol. 4. Socialization, personality, and social development* (pp. 643-691). New York: John Wiley.

Elliott, E. S., & Dweck, C. S. (1988). Goals: An approach to motivation and achievement. *Journal of Personality and Social Psychology, 54,* 5-12.

Emmer, E. T., Evertson, C. M., Clements, B. S., & Worsham, M. E. (2000). *Classroom management for secondary teachers* (5th ed.). Boston: Allyn & Bacon.

Epstein, J. L. (1989). Family structures and student motivation: A developmental perspective. In C. Ames & R. Ames (Eds.), *Research on motivation in education: Vol. 3. Goals and cognitions.* San Diego, CA: Academic Press.

Evertson, C. M., Emmer, E. T., Clements, B. S., & Worsham, M. E. (2000). *Classroom management for elementary teachers* (5th ed.). Boston: Allyn & Bacon.

Fogarty, R. (1997). *Problem-based learning and other curriculum models for the multiple intelligences classroom.* Arlington Heights, IL: IRI/Skylight Training & Publishing.

Gage, N. L., & Berliner, D. C. (1998). *Educational psychology* (6th ed.). Boston: Houghton Mifflin.

Gall, M. D., Gall, J. P., Jacobsen, D. R., & Bullock, T. L. (1990). *Tools for learning: A guide to teaching study skills.* Alexandria, VA: Association for Supervision & Curriculum Development.

Gardner, T. (1985). *Frames of mind: The theory of multiple intelligences.* New York: Basic Books.

Glasser, W. (1992). *The quality school: Managing students without coercion.* New York: HarperPerennial.

Good, T. L., & Brophy, J. E. (1995). *Contemporary educational psychology* (5th ed.). New York: Longman.

Good, T. L., & Brophy, J. E. (2000). *Looking in classrooms* (8th ed.). New York: Longman.

Good, T. L., Slavings, R., Harel, K., & Emerson, H. (1987). Student passivity: A study of question-asking in K-12 classrooms. *Sociology of Education, 60,* 181-199.

Reeve, J. M. (1996). *Motivating others: Nurturing inner motivational resources.* Boston: Allyn & Bacon.

Robbins, S. P. (1997). *Essentials of organizational behavior* (5th ed.). Englewood Cliffs, NJ: Prentice Hall.

Rosenholtz, S. J., & Simpson, C. (1984). The formation of ability conceptions: Developmental trend or social construction? *Review of Educational Research, 54,* 31-63.

Schunk, D. (1985). Self-efficacy and classroom learning. *Psychology in the Schools, 22,* 208-223.

Schunk, D. (1989). Self-efficacy and cognitive skill learning. In C. Ames & R. Ames (Eds.), *Research on motivation in education* (Vol. 3, pp. 13-44). San Diego, CA: Academic Press.

Shrigley, R. L. (1985). Curbing student disruption in the classroom: Teachers need intervention skills. *National Association of Secondary School Principals Bulletin, 69*(479), 26-32.

Slavin, R. E. (1997). *Educational psychology: Theory and practice* (5th ed.). Boston: Allyn & Bacon.

Spaulding, C. L. (1992). *Motivation in the classroom.* New York: McGraw-Hill.

Stipek, D. J. (1996). Motivation and instruction. In D. C. Berliner & R. C. Calfee (Eds.), *Handbook of educational psychology* (pp. 85-113). New York: Macmillan.

Stipek, D. J. (1998). *Motivation to learn: From theory to practice* (3rd ed.). Boston: Allyn & Bacon.

Svinicki, M. D. (1991). Practical implications of cognitive theories. In R. J. Menges & M. D. Svinicki (Eds.), *College teaching: From theory to practice* (pp. 27-37). San Francisco: Jossey-Bass.

Thompson, C., & Rudolph, L. (1992). *Counseling children* (3rd ed.). Pacific Grove, CA: Brooks/Cole.

Weiner, B. (1979). A theory of motivation for some classroom experiences. *Journal of Educational Psychology, 71,* 3-25.

Weinstein, C. S. (1996). *Secondary classroom management: Lessons from research and practice.* New York: McGraw-Hill.

Weinstein, C. S., & Mignano, A. J., Jr. (1997). *Elementary classroom management: Lessons from research and practice* (2nd ed.). New York: McGraw-Hill.

Wlodkowski, R. J. (1984). *Motivation and teaching: A practical guide.* Washington, DC: National Education Association.

Zimmerman, B. J. (1989). A social cognitive view of self-regulated academic learning. *Journal of Educational Psychology, 81,* 329-339.

Name Index

153

Subject Index